THE MAGIC OF MODERN ART
How to Love Modern & Contemporary Art

Robyn Jamison, MFA

To Carol—
My talented, beloved friend
of many years. Your friendship
is a treasure. I hope you enjoy this
book and that it opens up even
more of the magic of modern
and contemporary art for you!
Much love,
Robyn 6/5/22

Paperback ISBN 979-8-9853699-1-5

Library of Congress Control Number: 2021924976

First paperback edition March, 2022

Edited by Carol Winkler
Cover art by Antonio Manega
Layout by Antonio Manega
Author photograph by JD Swiger

Excerpts from interviews with art professionals printed by permission.

Reproductions of artists' work printed by permission.

Printed by The Robyn Jamison Company in Canada.

To my parents, Oscar and Norma Goldfarb

This book is your legacy.
It's a tribute to the heart and soul you put into parenting me.

The sacrifices you made for the sake of nurturing my artistic talents and
your dreams of what would be possible for me have been, I say, fulfilled.

You gave me a great life in the face of great challenges and made sure that
I had a foundation that would launch me into a life worth living.

Your hearts live in my heart.

The inspiration for writing this book came to me many years ago.

Fresh out of art school at the University of Kansas in 1975, I moved to Fort Worth, Texas and took a position as a guard at the Fort Worth Art Museum (now the Modern Art Museum of Fort Worth). That little museum had recruited a pre-eminent curator, Richard Koshalek, away from The Walker Art Center in Minneapolis. It was a real coup! Thanks to Mr. Koshalek's curating, our museum boasted exhibits that were noteworthy for both their progressiveness and their importance. I found it thrilling to work there.

As I stood guard in the galleries, I couldn't help but overhear the comments made by the museum guests. Unfortunately, in addition to the expected "oohs," "aahs," delighted dialogues and reverent silences, I was also privy to a disheartening number of disdainful, disbelieving and dispirited remarks. I can't count the number of people who grumbled, "My five-year-old could do that," or "I don't get it." Their frustration was palpable; it seemed to thicken the air.

Here's the thing that really got me about the disgruntled visitors. These were the people who were actually coming to see the art! They were the ones who had chosen to spend their precious time visiting the art museum.

What about the people who didn't come at all? I suspected that they must have been even more put off by Modern Art than those who showed up at the museum and denounced the art.

I was crystal clear (and still am) that Modern Art is a treasure trove of experiential wonder. In fact—and this is key—the very aspects of the art of our time that many people find most objectionable are the same aspects that, when seen from a different perspective, make this art so profoundly moving.

I vowed back then to do something to remedy this sad state of affairs. I set out to find a way to give people what they need in order to get in touch with that part of themselves that naturally resonates with the unique world of Modern and Contemporary Art.

To that end, I began an experiment I affectionately called "The Robyn Jamison Art Tours." I escorted groups of friends to Modern Art exhibits and, rather than deliver lectures about the art, I encouraged my friends to simply be with the art and let the art speak to them. I also posed thought-provoking questions for them to consider.

Every single one of them reported having had a breakthrough in their relationship with Modern Art, so I could tell I was on the right track. Although this was encouraging, my ultimate goal was to reach a much larger audience.

After having proved that my method worked—both in opening up Modern Art to people and opening people up to Modern Art—I decided that the way to give the gift of Modern Art to the most people in the shortest time was to write a book.

Not long after that, I began writing this book. I stopped and restarted it more times than I care to admit. I was unsure whether the book should be more academic. I was uncertain about whether to talk about specific works of art or just about Modern and Contemporary Art in general. I doubted that I was qualified to write this book since I wasn't a famous artist or the curator of a major museum.

On top of that, this poor book lived through a variety of titles over the years. My favorite of the discarded titles is "Art Savvy 101." I might have kept that title had the "101" thing not become a cliché before I got around to finishing this book!

It was when I turned 65 and was taking stock of my life that I understood that if this book was going to get done, it was up to me. I took it on as my legacy to get this message out to the world while I still had time.

Once I had a good part of the book under way and had found the perfect writing partner in Carol Winkler, I realized that the book is only part of what I'm up to. Back when I was working in that museum and got the inspiration to write this book, I had imagined much more than just writing a book. I had originally envisioned being a spokesperson for Modern Art.

I never forgot all I'd hoped to accomplish, but, having bought into our cultural beliefs about age, I thought it was too late. Silly me.

In the spring of 2020, I attended the Conference for Global Transformation, hosted by Landmark Worldwide. At that event there were hundreds of people who were successfully addressing major global issues. I was inspired to go beyond merely writing this book; I made a commitment to do everything in my power to fulfill my original vision.

I'm now spearheading a movement that is dedicated to bringing about:

A world where everyone everywhere experiences
the magic and wonder of Modern and Contemporary Art.

In short, I am a champion for the difference that this art makes in people's lives.

For more information, I invite you to go to www.MagicOfModernArt.com. You can subscribe to the site to be informed of new blog posts and events. Also, please feel free to contact me directly at Robyn@MagicOf-ModernArt.com. If you are interested in getting involved, let's have a conversation.

ACKNOWLEDGEMENTS

This book would not be what it is without the contributions of so many generous, brilliant people along the way. To name just a few . . .

Otto Fox ~ my dream-guy husband and number one fan. Long before I found Otto, I envisioned a marriage that would be like a springboard from which each of us could learn, grow and accomplish. I'm forever grateful to be living that dream.

Carol Winkler ~ a full partner in every single aspect of the global commitment, The Magic of Modern Art. Her facility with words, organized mind and relentless stand all combine to bring the magic of a perfect collaboration to this project.

Renee McGivern ~ my go-to wizard for questions great and small. She talked me off more ledges than I can count with her ingenious, unselfishly-given counsel.

Meryl Sher ~ who so graciously took on the considerable task of proofing and refining this book. Her eagle-eyed precision and fine sensibilities provided just the right finishing touches.

Anthony Schmitt ~ to whom I made promises week after week for what I would accomplish. Not only did he keep me on the straight and narrow, but he also dropped nourishing morsels of wisdom all along the way.

Becky Hendrick ~ a fellow artist, author and teacher, who encouraged and cheered me on. Her beautifully-written book, Getting It: A Guide to Understanding and Appreciating Art, served as an inspiration for this one.

Rabbi Raine Teller ~ a friend with a heart of gold. It was her magnanimous gift that allowed me to write this book with no concern for the means to publish it.

Mark Ramon ~ his can-do professionalism combined with his mind-reading capabilities, patience and good-heartedness made him the most perfect web designer and technical guy on planet Earth.

Antonio Manega ~ the experience of working with him was the ideal blend of creativity and collaboration. And, voilà! Designs for this project that went beyond what I envisioned.

The Magic of Modern Art Mensches ~ a talented, passionate group of art lovers who have supported this book and its broader mission with unabashed enthusiasm. Being with them has enlivened and sustained me.

The inspirational art professionals I interviewed ~ their openness and passion for Modern Art breathed fire into this book. It was an absolute joy to be in their presence!

Lastly, all my past and present influences ~ teachers, mentors, authors, artists and just plain amazing friends. In giving of themselves so generously and with such genius, they sowed the seeds that blossomed into this book and the overarching commitment that everyone everywhere experience the magic and wonder of Modern Art.

From the bottom of my heart...thank you!

CONTENTS

The principle of true art
is not to portray, but to evoke.
— Jerzy Kosinski

This book's mission is simple—to offer everyone the opportunity to become as wild about Modern Art as I am. I am committed that this book provide what you need so that your visits to Modern Art exhibits become joyful, enriching experiences—experiences that you eagerly anticipate, avidly soak in and never get over. In short, I wrote this book so you can have the magic of Modern Art in your life!

I assert that the ability to appreciate art, including Modern Art, is innate to all human beings. I have discovered that unlocking this natural love of art has much more to do with clearing out what's in the way than it does with accumulating information.

When I inquire into my own love affair with Modern Art, I see clearly that when I am focused entirely on the art in front of me—setting aside judgment and cognitive thinking—that's when I find myself profoundly moved and deeply satisfied.

I have come to the conclusion that the key to unlocking the magic of Modern Art is in the ability to immerse oneself in the art and truly "experience" it. So the obvious and most vital question becomes, "How does one learn to experience Modern Art?" That, dear reader, is the work of this book.

How This Book Is Organized

Part One is about opening up the possibility of falling in love with Modern Art. We will delve into the specific benefits of having a great relationship with Modern Art. This is the "why bother" conversation of the book. Once you are clear that there's an enormously rich experience awaiting you when you connect with Modern Art, I believe you will be convinced that making this connection is well worth your time and effort.

I will also make the case that everyone has a natural affinity for Modern Art. Unfortunately, many of us have become disconnected from this affinity, due to "stuff" that has gotten in the way. It could be stuff from the past like clueless art teachers, snooty museum staffers and even the seeming weirdness and inaccessibility of Modern Art itself. Part One ends with an invitation for you to make a declaration—a declaration that you're willing to re-open yourself to all that Modern Art has to offer.

In Part Two, I will reveal and debunk the misconceptions that could be preventing you from experiencing the magnificence of Modern Art. We will tackle the various beliefs that might be keeping you and Modern Art at arm's length. Completing this process will forever alter what's possible for you with Modern Art.

Part Three is about seeing art through new eyes. I will discuss the notion of "context" and show you that you already have a context for Modern Art. This context has been underlying (or even sabotaging) every aspect of your relationship to Modern Art. You will invent a new context that empowers and inspires you. With this new context under your belt, you'll be ready to explore some creative ways to approach your Modern Art viewing. I will share with you The Magic of Modern Art Tour, which I have found invaluable for introducing people to the magic of Modern Art.

I devote the last chapter in Part Three to excerpts from interviews I conducted with a variety of artists and art professionals. These Modern Art lovers will let you in on how they think and feel about Modern Art, giving you insight into ways to maximize your own precious art-viewing time. Those of them who are artists were generous enough to allow me to include examples of their extraordinary work.

Part Four is about developing your art savvy and deepening your relationship with Modern Art. I begin with a brief history of Modern Art, then delve into some invaluable art rudiments with an eye toward expanding your ability to explore Modern Art with confidence.

In Part Five, I cover the topic of curating your own art collection. For many of us, choosing, arranging, hanging and caring for our art is a mystery. This section is devoted to giving you the basic know-how to collect art that you love and display it with aplomb.

An Important Note on the Use of the Terms "Art" and "Modern" in This Book

When I talk about art in this book, I mean the kind of art that is displayed in museums and fine galleries. Such art is sometimes referred to as "serious art," "fine" art," or "art with a capital A." It's the kind of art that has the potential to stretch you, transport you and have a profound, lasting impact on you.

In the art world, there are certain terms that are not always used the same way. Among these are "Modern," "Contemporary," and "Avant-garde." In this book, I use "modern" as a catch-all term meant to include Modern Art, Contemporary Art and beyond. This is similar to its use in "The Museum of Modern Art (MoMA)" and some other museums that show modern and contemporary art.

For example, MoMA's description of its collection implies a broad use of the term, "modern."

> MoMA's rich and varied collection offers a panoramic overview of modern and contemporary art, from the innovative European painting and sculpture of the 1880s to today's film, design, and performance art.

As you read this book, bear in mind that "Modern" is used in a very broad way.

A Final Thought

Whether you have a strong background in art or consider yourself a novice, there's no question that you have a natural affinity for art. Were this not the case, art would have been a passing fancy, not the sustained abiding presence it has been throughout human history.

Loving Modern Art does not require intensive study or memorization of data or positive thinking or trying to talk yourself into anything. All it takes is your desire to have the magic of Modern Art in your life and the willingness to let this book be your guide.

Here's to many magical hours with Modern Art!

*Art enables us to find ourselves
and lose ourselves at the same time.*
                    — Thomas Merton

PART ONE

Opening up the Possibility

CHAPTER 1   MODERN ART – WHAT'S IN IT FOR YOU

The first order of business is to let you know why it's worth your while to become a fan of Modern Art.

Immersing ourselves in art opens the door to an exquisite, indescribable phenomenon that is undeniably personal and profoundly moving. Some of us describe it as transcendent or spiritual. It's an experience that puts us in a state of reverence and awe.

Although every genre and era of art has the ability to affect us deeply, Modern Art, particularly the most recent, is unique in that it is a reflection of contemporary economic, political and cultural influences. It offers new perspectives, enhances awareness and serves as a catalyst for inspired action.

Moreover, fully appreciating Modern Art requires a greater amount of participation on the part of the audience than does art of earlier eras. Although you can glance at Modern Art and write it off, you cannot glance at Modern Art and get it. This, in and of itself, suggests that Modern Art offers a deeper, richer, more engaging experience than the art of previous periods.

I am clear that the power of Modern Art lies in the way it touches us. While the benefits are too many to mention, here are some of my favorites.

- When you are immersed in it, you have that lovely feeling of "being in the zone."
- Your visceral responses to it can be a source of surprise and delight.
- Spending time in a space dedicated to it clears your head and refreshes your spirit.
- The sensory experience of being with it is a catalyst for personal growth.
- Your emotional responses to it bring about insights into yourself.
- Being in the presence of it stimulates your own creativity.
- The effects of being with it linger and lead to a sense of awakening that unfolds over time.
- Being in the presence of it has a significant positive effect on your well-being.
- The beauty of it transports you into a space of awe and wonder.
- It's intellectually stimulating to engage with visual expressions that are so provocatively presented.
- Opening yourself up to an artist's viewpoint broadens your perspective.

So far, I have been describing the remarkable experiential benefits of Modern Art. Equally impressive are those benefits that have been revealed through scientific research, especially those pertaining to our well-being and the quality of our lives.*

Scientists have learned that the act of simply looking at art leads to measurable increases in both cognitive and emotional intelligence. They have also discovered significant reductions in stress and improvements in physical well-being—specifically in normalizing heart rate, blood pressure and cortisol levels. What's more, they found that looking at art brings about increased activity in the specific brain systems that underlie the conscious processing of new information and give it meaning.

In studies where participants viewed artwork that they found to be particularly beautiful or awe-inspiring, the hormone dopamine was immediately released into their brains. Dopamine is directly related to feelings of love, pleasure and desire. What's more, researchers found that the feeling of awe leads to an enhanced sense of hope and fulfillment.

How Might These Benefits Show Up in Your Life?

Picture this scenario. You start visiting a Modern Art exhibit once a week over your lunch hour. Each time, you return to work refreshed and clear-headed, and, as a result, you get a raise or a promotion!

What if the de-stressing you experience from your visits to local galleries allows you to bring cooperation to your team of rugged individualists?

Imagine what your relationship with your sweetheart would be like, if, thanks to taking in Modern Art together on Sunday afternoons, you were to become happier and more relaxed.

Suppose you and your partner go to a Modern Art opening. Over dinner afterward, your partner talks to you about some aspect of your personality that you have been denying and you are suddenly able to see their point of view.

What might your life be like if your body were producing more of the happiness hormone, dopamine?

What if your creativity were to skyrocket? What difference would that make in the big project you're spear-heading? Or you suddenly think of creative ways to support your shy five-year-old in participating in the school play?

You could live longer just by spending time with Modern Art! Remember, it normalizes your blood pressure, heart rate, and cortisol levels.

Are these scenarios unrealistic? Not in the least.

*The vast majority of the research I encountered assessed the benefits received from viewing all art, not only Modern Art. Additionally, some of the studies were inclusive of all the arts, not just visual art. See References and Resources at the end of the book.

Appreciating Art Is in Our Nature

I firmly believe that appreciating art is in our nature—intrinsic to us as human beings. In fact, there are many respected and credible experts in the field who share the view that appreciating art is a universal human instinct. Some of them have even concluded that our brains are hardwired to appreciate art.

Empirical evidence in the form of art objects that have been produced by every culture and civilization abounds. Equally compelling is the fact that nearly all young children delight in colors, shapes, forms and textures.

In my case, I grew up in St. Louis, Missouri, in the 1950s. In those days, art held a prominent place in public schools. I fondly remember our wonderful grade school field trips to the St. Louis Art Museum, which was (and still is) an excellent art museum.

I'll never forget what it was like to visit the art museum for the first time. I was ecstatic to discover there was a whole huge building devoted solely to art!

When I was first introduced to the world of art, I was most attracted to the art of the Renaissance period—Da Vinci, Michelangelo, Raphael, Donatello. Those artists' technical command of realism and the intense feeling that their paintings, drawings and sculptures were able to convey took my breath away.

Appreciating Modern Art Is Also in Our Nature

Since appreciating art is in our nature, doesn't it follow that the same is true for Modern Art?

Maybe your comfort zone ends at Impressionism or some other art movement or era. The same or even greater enjoyment that you currently experience with your favorite art is available with all Modern Art.

Here's how I got in touch with my affinity for Modern Art. As a child, I was exposed to reproductions of Modern Art, mostly in books. They didn't have much impact on me. I held fast to my preference for the "Old Masters."

It wasn't until I saw a major Vincent Van Gogh retrospective at the St. Louis Art Museum that all this changed. When I caught sight of the actual paintings hanging on the museum walls, I was awestruck. The colors were so vivid, the brushstrokes so bold—to me, those paintings epitomized vitality itself. I found myself completely overtaken by the sensations those paintings evoked in me. I had no awareness of anything else. It was as if I had disappeared and there was only the experience of those paintings.

That extraordinary Van Gogh exhibition was a turning point in my life. I was 12 years old. That show opened me up to all the innovative art of the late 1800s and beyond. Along with that came the realization that art doesn't have to be realistic to be moving and powerful. A whole new realm of art appreciation opened up to me.

Edgar Degas' delicate dancers, Toulouse Lautrec's gaudy performers, Gauguin's exotic Tahitian women, Pablo Picasso and George Braque's cubist explorations, Dali's dreamlike surrealism. A kaleidoscope of endless visual possibilities was now mine! I didn't know much about the theory behind all the art movements, but I was inspired by the seemingly endless expressions of creativity.

It doesn't matter whether you are, as I was at first, only comfortable with the Old Masters. I return to my original assertion: Appreciating art is in our nature, intrinsic to us as human beings. Furthermore, I assert that our affinity for art is not exclusive; it's inclusive. Appreciating Modern Art is in our nature.

If You Don't Experience an Affinity for Modern Art

I was one of the lucky ones. Nothing ever came between me and my natural affinity for art. Sadly, that's not the case for everyone. For some of us, this connection seems to have disappeared altogether. Where did it go? I say it's still there, lying dormant, ready to be reawakened.

Maybe you're among those who are comfortable with the art of earlier eras but simply can't relate to Modern Art. Your lack of resonance with Modern Art could be the result of painful past experiences. Or, it could simply be due to a lack of familiarity and exposure to it. If people around you weren't fans of Modern Art, you might have taken on their point of view. Navigating one's relationship with Modern Art can be thorny regardless of your past history with it.

With its myriad of outside-the-box expressions, Modern Art might not fit your expectations of what art is or what art is supposed to be. So it's no surprise that Modern Art can seem completely incomprehensible.

Question: What do we humans typically do when confronted with something we don't understand?
Answer: We try to figure it out.
Question: What do we do if we can't figure it out?
Answer: Avoid it. Or invalidate it. Maybe invalidate ourselves. Or possibly give up altogether.

There, in a nutshell, is how so many of us relate (or don't relate) to Modern Art. We avoid it, invalidate it and become resigned that we will never get it.

Some of us have developed sophisticated strategies to alleviate our discomfort with Modern Art. Instead of admitting (even to ourselves) that we're intimidated by it, we come up with excuses. "I'm too busy to attend that art show," or "I'm too tired." Rather than expressing our fear that we'll never get Modern Art, we feign indifference. "So what if I don't like Modern Art?" or, "Modern Art? I can take it or leave it."

There is a certain level of comfort in avoiding the issue altogether. Being comfortable is so much easier than taking risks. In opting for comfort, we don't have to confront our lack of art savvy or struggle to comprehend art that seems alien to us.

Truth be told, settling for comfort would be just fine if it weren't for the fact that we are, by nature, profoundly and inherently connected to art. Modern Art is no exception. It is natural for us to resonate with the art of our own time, the art that reflects contemporary thinking and contemporary issues. When we shun Modern Art, we cut ourselves off from a vital aspect of our culture and our nature.

The Way Forward

Reawakening your innate appreciation for Modern Art is not as difficult as you would imagine. Even if you've spent years relying on the various avoidance strategies you have cultivated, it's still possible to cause a shift for yourself. Even if you have minimized the risks and turned away from Modern Art altogether, it's not too late!

The entry point is to become aware of the fact that you yourself have shut the door on Modern Art. This may seem counterintuitive and daunting to confront. Unsettling though this realization might seem, this is, in fact, good news. Once you realize it was you who shut the door in the first place, guess what? You also recognize that you have the power to re-open that door and reclaim your affinity for Modern Art.

Re-opening that door requires your willingness to make yourself available for all that Modern Art has to offer. Without the willingness, the door remains shut. With the willingness, you're well on your way to reawakening your natural affinity for Modern Art.

Once you're willing to open the door to Modern Art, the next step is to say so, to declare it. Making a declaration has a unique and powerful impact. When you declare something, you literally bring that thing into existence. When the umpire shouts, "You're out!"—you're out! Likewise, the very instant you declare that you are willing, you're willing.

It takes courage to re-open yourself to any aspect of your life where you've shut the door. Re-opening yourself to Modern Art is no exception. I encourage you to take the plunge. Make the declaration that you are now open to reap the benefits inherent in Modern Art!

Don't be surprised if you experience a shift in your relationship to Modern Art just by making this declaration. You may feel more relaxed and curious about it. You might find yourself ready to go see some Modern Art!

Wherever you are at this point, read on! The following chapters are devoted to freeing you from old ideas that run counter to your newly declared openness.

*Art washes away from the soul the dust
of everyday life.*

— Pablo Picasso

PART TWO

Identifying and Dispelling Counterproductive Beliefs

CHAPTER 3   BELIEFS – WHAT HAVE THEY GOT TO DO WITH IT?

Here's some good news. You don't need to amass a mountain of information to have the magic of Modern Art in your life. In fact, it's mostly a matter of unlearning—of letting go of those beliefs that might be making you feel like an outsider to Modern Art.

When we think about our beliefs (consider "beliefs" to include all those opinions and judgments we hold to be true), I suspect that most of us tend to focus only on our significant beliefs. We think about our beliefs about spirituality, religion or politics—about family, education and health care.

However, when we really look, it becomes clear that we have beliefs about almost everything, including relatively trivial stuff such as the best brand of toothpaste or the right color to paint a kitchen.

Personally, I have many beliefs about art and Modern Art:

- I believe art is one of the highest expressions of humanity;
- I believe art is a unifying force;
- I believe that being able to relate to Modern Art is an important aspect of being a well-rounded person;
- I believe valuing art and artists is essential for a civilization to thrive.

When I was younger, I assumed these beliefs were self-evident. This assumption was reinforced in art school, where I was immersed in a world filled entirely with artists and aspiring artists. We were like-minded; we shared many of the same beliefs about art. I had grown accustomed to being around people who loved Modern Art, and it seemed like an "of course" that everyone loved it as much as I did.

In the preface, I shared that I received a crash course in reality the moment I left art school and entered the workforce. In my first job as a museum guard, I was privy to the surprisingly diverse range of comments made by museum guests. Perhaps it was because I had just emerged from an environment where we all valued Modern Art so much that the disgruntled mutterings came as such a shock to me.

I was stunned the first time I heard a museum visitor exclaim, "My five-year-old could do that!" She was looking at a famous work by Joan Miro. I had just spent five years of intensive work developing my talent and skills, and I knew beyond a shadow of a doubt that no five-year-old could produce the refinement and compositional brilliance of such a deceptively simple masterpiece.

I asked myself, "Why would anyone express disdain for such a marvelous work of art?" One thing seemed certain—alienated museum-goers could not have been seeing the art the same way I did. I wondered what prevented them from recognizing how great the art was. Then, as I listened to more and more similar comments, it became apparent that these frustrated art viewers had firmly-held beliefs about what art should be about and how it should look. There was no question that the art they were seeing failed to meet those criteria.

I loved most of the works we showed at the museum and appreciated those I didn't love. Yet, those same exhibits were totally unappealing to so many other people. It would be easy just to say, "Oh well, each to his own." But what about all the evidence pointing to the fact that appreciating art is intrinsic to our nature? Why would that apply only to certain art genres or periods?

Something else had to be in play for those dissatisfied museum-goers. As far as I could tell, it was those strongly-held opinions—opinions that invalidated Modern Art in their minds. What if those beliefs were at the heart of what prevented those people from appreciating Modern Art?

The Power of Beliefs

To give you a sense of the incredible power that beliefs have and their ability to shape our world, I want to provide you with an example from my own life.

When, at age 18, it came time for me to choose my college major, my parents demanded that I get a degree in art education rather than a straight degree in visual art. They didn't think I could make a living as an artist. They insisted I have something to "fall back on." Although I outwardly resisted their point of view, their fears began working on me. Before I knew it, the belief, "Artists are doomed to either starve or sell out," began to lodge itself in my subconscious. I acquiesced to my parents' wishes and enrolled in the Art Education program.

Once in college, I discovered, to my dismay, that I was no longer a big fish in a little pond; I had become a little fish in a big sea. I was surrounded by hundreds of other art students, all of whom had been the "class artists" in their respective schools just as I had been in mine. I'd had no idea that art at the university level would be so competitive.

To top it all off, not only had so many of my artist and non-artist friends bought into the myth of the "starving artist," but the world at large seemed to believe it as well. With so many people believing it, it had to be true, right? After all, "the starving artist" is a cliché known to just about everyone.

By the time I graduated from college, I didn't even consider setting up shop to earn a living with my art. Nope. I worked at an odd assortment of jobs, only some of which were even vaguely art-related. Making art had become relegated to a hobby.

If you had asked me then, "Why aren't you making a living with your art?" I would have recited my long litany on "how it is" for artists and that my only choices were (yes, you guessed it) to be a starving artist, sell out, or change professions. The last thing I would have considered at that point was the possibility that the belief itself was the culprit.

To my great good fortune, at age 29, I participated in an extremely impactful personal development seminar where I discovered that believing something doesn't make it true—that, even if the majority of people believe something, it still doesn't mean that it's true.

Once I had this realization, it was a short leap to let go of my disempowering belief that all artists are doomed to starve, sell out or switch professions. A whole new world of possibility opened up for me as an artist.

At the time I took the seminar, I happened to be working as a writer and editor in a small freelance writing firm. When I returned to my job on the Monday following the seminar weekend, my boss informed me that he had accepted a lucrative position at a well-known advertising agency. He offered me his entire business—lock, stock and client base!

Had he made this offer a few days earlier, I would have gratefully accepted it. However, I was in a different state of mind as a result of the seminar. So, I thanked him profusely for his generous offer and graciously declined, explaining that I was going to pursue my passion—art.

I began my art career the very next day. I went on to enjoy a successful twelve-year run of creating hundreds of one-of-a-kind ceramic pieces that I sold through galleries and private commissions. Just by dispelling one significant belief, a whole new future was mine.

How Beliefs Work

Before I get into the specific counterproductive beliefs that may be keeping you alienated from Modern Art, I'd like to explain how beliefs work in general. Remember, "beliefs" include all those opinions and judgments we consider to be true.

We acquire beliefs in two main ways. We inherit them and we invent them.

Our inherited beliefs are passed down to us through our parents, teachers, clergy, relatives, friends, advertising and even from society as a whole. For example, I inherited the belief that education is a major priority in life. I can't remember ever not knowing that I was destined to go to college. This is just one personal example from the mountain of beliefs we have all inherited.

When we invent beliefs, we do so both consciously and unconsciously in order to make sense of the world. As a young child, I believed that the majority of the world's population was Jewish. This makes sense if you know that I was raised in a community made up almost entirely of Jewish people. I knew about people of other religions and ethnicities, but I was surrounded by Jewish people. I never thought to ask whether we were the majority in the world and don't recall a specific moment when I created that belief. I didn't think of it as a belief, but just something I thought was true. That's how it goes with beliefs.

Whether inherited or invented, once we adopt a particular belief, it often operates in the background calling the shots. We rarely question that belief—in fact, we become attached to it. Our actions and our speaking line up with it. We collect evidence that supports it and we ignore, fail to notice, or even refuse to consider anything that flies in the face of it.

Nonetheless, beliefs are not set in stone; they are malleable. But since many of them are in the background, we are totally unaware of them, let alone conscious of their impact. In order to gain access to our beliefs, we must bring them from the background of our consciousness to the foreground. Once we're aware of their existence, they loosen their grip. We then have the choice to let go of those beliefs that no longer serve us.

Just to be clear, there are ultimately no right or wrong beliefs. However, there are beliefs that interfere with the ability to appreciate Modern Art. From this point forward, I will refer to these as "Counterproductive Beliefs."

In the next few chapters, I'm going to expose the mischief inherent in a number of these Counterproductive Beliefs—beliefs about art, artists, the art world and even about you. I suggest you read through them and put a check mark beside any that apply to you. Every Counterproductive Belief you recognize and dispel takes you another step closer to the endgame—becoming wild about Modern Art.

CHAPTER 4   COUNTERPRODUCTIVE BELIEFS – THEY'RE ABOUT US

I have my own "look." I wear my hair very short and usually have a streak of bright red, blue or purple in it. My style of dress leans toward the avant-garde and I always wear a pair (or a mixed pair) of earrings out of my extensive collection of handcrafted earrings.

Complete strangers frequently ask me if I'm an artist. When they learn that I am, they tell me, all too often, "Oh, I don't know anything about art." If we have more time to visit, I ask them to elaborate. They usually tell me stories that explain their lack of involvement with art. Their stories revolve around being too busy, too occupied with other activities or lacking the background, inclination, or aptitude that dovetails with the world of art.

On the surface, these stories illustrate valid reasons for a lack of involvement with art. But when we consider the fact that we all have a natural affinity for art, it becomes apparent that something else is at play.

Over the years, I've had many opportunities to probe further when people have shared their reasons for not engaging with art. Their answers almost invariably reveal an underlying belief (or set of beliefs) that goes something like this: "I'm not the kind of person who's meant to have art in my life." Said another way, "There's something about me that doesn't fit with the world of art."

This chapter focuses on those Counterproductive Beliefs that we have about ourselves—beliefs that stop us from appreciating art, especially Modern Art. I find them to be the most problematic of all the Counterproductive Beliefs because they act as gatekeepers, denying us access to the world of art before we can even get started with it.

In my experience, among those beliefs we have about ourselves, the following two are most ubiquitous.

☐ Modern Art Is Not for People Like Me

You may relate to one or more of the following premises underlying this belief:

- I'm not smart enough;
- I'm not sophisticated enough;
- I don't fit in with the Modern Art crowd; or
- There must be some mysterious "something" that I lack.

There is a fundamental assumption that keeps this belief in place, which is, "Modern Art is only accessible to a certain type of person." Given that, it's no wonder that so few of us feel at home with Modern Art.

Let me assist you in putting this belief to rest.

Simply put, it's not even remotely true that Modern Art is for just one type of person. I know countless Modern Art lovers, and I assure you that they come in all ages, ethnicities, genders, professions, nationalities and educational backgrounds.

Furthermore, you have already been introduced to the notion that appreciating art. which includes Modern Art, is intrinsic to all of us as human beings. That means that everyone (including you) has a natural affinity for Modern Art.

So, any way you look at it, Modern Art is for everyone, with no one left out!

☐ I Don't Trust My Experience of Modern Art

You may feel so far out of your depth with Modern Art that it seems like a complete mystery to you—and not the fun kind of mystery. If you feel this way, being in the presence of Modern Art can be massively uncomfortable. You certainly have an experience in the presence of the art, but you just don't trust it.

So, there you are, actually experiencing something in response to the art. But meanwhile, the little voice in your head is telling you that you have no idea what you're doing. This voice keeps you from trusting your experience, and more importantly, from truly enjoying Modern Art.

Do you see the irony? The problem is not your actual responses to the art, but rather the second-guessing that goes on when you lack confidence in your experience. It's crazy-making!

But wait, there's more. Your lack of trust in the validity of your own personal experience will drive you to seek relief. Often, our go-to source for relief is answers. I suspect that it's this mechanism—this drive to alleviate our discomfort by finding answers—that prompts us to seek out some authority or set of rules.

Here's the deal. The joy of art lives in your personal, unique experience of it. When it comes to art, there is no absolute truth. There's no certain thing you're supposed to get.

It may be true that you would benefit from more exposure and guidance when it comes to viewing art. However, in no way does that diminish the fact that you have an experience—your personal experience—in the presence of art. And your experience is valid, valid, valid!

Letting go of these Counterproductive Beliefs about yourself opens a fundamental door into the world of Modern Art.

CHAPTER 5   COUNTERPRODUCTIVE BELIEFS – ALL THOSE RULES

When I went to undergraduate art school in the early 1970s, art was heavily influenced by an art critic named Clement Greenberg (1909-1994). According to him, art should not be representational. Naturally, my professors were influenced by what was happening in the art world, so our class critiques reflected the views of Clement Greenberg. (The painting style that conformed to these parameters is often called "formalism" because it's all about the form—the shapes, colors, design and so on.)

Fast forward to 1981. I had begun creating one-of-a-kind ceramic pieces for a living. I spent most of my time sequestered in my studio making art. I was selling my work privately and wasn't paying much attention to the developments in the art world. After twelve years of this, I felt the pull of my first love, painting, and decided to go back to school to get my Masters of Fine Arts degree. This was in 1993.

I remember my first class critique in graduate school like it was yesterday. I can recall what the room looked like and who was there. I was expecting the critique to be similar to the ones I had attended in undergraduate school. Instead, I was completely blindsided by the conversation.

Most of the student work being critiqued was representational. I was expecting the work to be criticized for not conforming to the parameters set by Clement Greenberg. Instead, there was a lively discussion that encompassed both the content and the formal aspects of the work. Unbeknownst to me, art theory had taken a huge turn. I felt like Rip Van Winkle! I had stepped into a new reality.

Without even realizing it, I had made it a rule that art should not depict things in the world—it should only be about such things as color, texture, brushstrokes, and movement. Art should be non-objective. I was a formalist.

It took a little time to adjust, but I got up to speed with the art theory of the time, which was (and still is today) much more inclusive of a wide range of artistic expressions.

Through all this, I learned a valuable lesson—a much broader lesson than just being reminded that art theory doesn't stand still. It became obvious to me that it was a mistake for me to use any set of rules as a justification for engaging with some art and rejecting the rest.

Based on my many years of experience observing and talking with people in museums and galleries, my educated guess is that you, dear reader, have your own set of rules which govern your acceptance or rejection of art. Unfortunately, these rules are bound to significantly diminish your art-viewing enjoyment.

The Counterproductive Belief below sets the tone for the rest of the Counterproductive Beliefs addressed in this chapter.

☐ There Are Definite, Fixed Rules Set by Some Absolute Authority That Determine Which Art Is Valid

Within this particular Counterproductive Belief, there are two distinct beliefs to unpack and debunk:

- There are definite, fixed rules that determine which art is valid; and,
- There is some absolute authority that determines which art is valid.

Let's tackle them one by one.

Regarding the first belief, there are no hard and fast rules about what makes good art. In fact, if you are looking for an art rulebook, you won't find one.

Adherence to the notion of definite, fixed rules has inadvertently wreaked all kinds of havoc in our relationship to art. Rather than being free to simply experience the art, we try to figure out whether it follows the rules and is worth our time. Fearing we might make some awkward faux pas and embarrass ourselves, we forfeit exploration and enjoyment in favor of caution and guardedness.

As to the second belief, the supposed existence of some absolute authority that determines the rules, there isn't one. There is no agreed-upon or unified body of experts that tells us what is and is not valid art.

There are, however, countless influential "experts"—writers, critics, curators, even organizations—that make pronouncements about what constitutes valid art. Such pronouncements are actually just opinions in disguise—subjective standards specifying the "shoulds and should nots" of legitimate art. Moreover, it's worth noting that these opinions often contradict each other. So much for a unified set of rules, let alone an absolute authority.

Given our human tendency to turn the opinions of experts into rules, it's no surprise that so many of us are limited by this particular Counterproductive Belief.

By the way, did you know that the Impressionists' first exhibition was met by outright disdain by the critics? Of course, today, Impressionism is widely accepted, even revered, and holds a prominent place in art history. We need look no further than this example to confirm the folly and fallibility in placing our trust in any authorities or set of rules.

For the sake of enjoying your art-viewing time to the max, I highly recommend that you put this Counterproductive Belief to rest and see what happens. I predict a fresh and exhilarating art-viewing experience.

☐ **The Only Art That's Valid Is in Museums or High-End Galleries**

Consider that just because art hasn't made its way into museums or high-end galleries doesn't mean that the art is lacking in any way. On the contrary, in many cases, its omission is simply a matter of fashion; galleries and museums favor the art that's popular at any given time.

Consider also that museums depend on money from the public, so they have to appeal to their market. And as for galleries, they are ultimately just retail stores, so their job is to offer the art that's selling.

There are many excellent artists—artists who produce art that's just as amazing as the art in museums and high-end galleries. Some of these artists prefer not to have their work exhibited in such venues for any number of reasons. They might not want to give up a high percentage of the sale price of their work. They might prefer to retain the right to sell their work themselves, which isn't possible with the vast majority of galleries, which demand exclusivity.

Other artists love to create art but don't love to do what it takes to sell it. Or they lack the skills to market their work. I think most of us are familiar with artists who are great at art but not at business.

If you think of any career or pursuit—in the arts or otherwise—you know that there are plenty of unsung stars and heroes. There's a ton of great art to be enjoyed outside of traditional exhibition spaces. Museums and high-end galleries don't have a monopoly on valid art.

☐ You're Supposed to Like All the Art You See in Museums and High-End Galleries

If you've ever been underwhelmed by the art you encountered in a museum or highly reputable gallery and thought something like, "I should like this art because look where it's being shown—but I don't like it, so I must be missing something," then you have this belief. You believe you're supposed to like all the art you see in museums and classy galleries.

Take heart. It's highly unlikely that you're going to like all the Modern Art you see. Your taste is your own and not to be discounted.

That said, I'm about to write something that isn't part of debunking this Counterproductive Belief. I think I would be remiss not to mention it. LIking and appreciating are not always the same. There is value in exploring Modern Art that you don't like. By exploring it, you may discover things about it that you appreciate or find interesting. This book is aimed at expanding your capacity to appreciate Modern Art.

So relax. It's okay that you don't like all the Modern Art you see in museums and high-end galleries. Guess what? Nobody does!

☐ Art Should Depict Real Life and the More Realistic It Looks, the Better It Is; All Other Art Is Inferior or Invalid

For many of us, this belief goes all the way back to childhood. The "class artists" were usually the ones who could draw and paint well, and "well" meant that they were the best at making realistic-looking pictures. Not only that, but it's likely that most of the art we were exposed to in grade school was representational. Naturally, we came to believe that realism is the holy grail of art.

In fact, through much of history, artists functioned as visual historians. They were charged with creating accurate likenesses of important people and events as well as illustrating the Church's doctrine. Think royal portraits, Mona Lisa and Sistine Chapel.

The advent of photography in the 1820s shifted the role of the artist dramatically. Cameras could do the work formerly delegated to artists. However, this did little to diminish the status of masterful realistic rendering.

Nonetheless, freed from the obligation to function as society's pictorial historians, artists found themselves with a whole new realm of possibilities to explore with their art.

In the late 1800s, the Impressionists experimented with, as they described it, "painting the light." It was a significant departure from tradition, setting the stage for other artists to invent new ways to think about art and new ways to approach its creation. The magnitude of this explosion of creativity cannot be overstated.

Inventiveness and the act of "pushing the creative envelope" became essential aspects of art-making. Sure, innovation in art has always been highly valued, but originality became king with the advent of this new freedom. It was no longer that artists could explore new territory but rather that they should.

By setting aside this Counterproductive Belief, you can step into the vast world of Modern Art. It will wow you with big swashes of color, subtle plays of light or shimmering kaleidoscopic imagery. It can also take you to a quiet place or challenge your thinking. Before you know it, you will find yourself transported to a world where wonder abounds.

☐ Every Work of Art Has a Specific, Fixed Meaning

I cannot count the number of times I've been asked, in reference to some work of art, "What does it mean?" Behind this question lies the assumption that every work of art has one meaning and that that meaning can be expressed in words.

This belief is hugely impactful—guaranteed to ruin your day at the art museum. Let's suppose that you believe every work of art has a fixed, specific meaning. You're likely to spend your art-viewing time going from one piece to the next, intent on discovering the "true meaning" of each one.

When you believe that every work of art has a fixed, specific meaning, you're bound to be disappointed or frustrated any time you fail to decipher that meaning. At other times, you may feel confident that you've broken the code and figured out what the artist intended.

Unfortunately, whether you end up frustrated and disappointed or certain and triumphant, your quest for resolution has been an empty one. You have invested a lot of thought and energy in a purely intellectual pursuit and possibly missed all the yumminess of just being present with the art.

Here's the bottom line regarding meaning in art. Art's ultimate power lies in its mystery, in its ability to provoke open-ended exploration. To single-mindedly pursue a fixed, specific meaning is to miss the fullness of the art experience and deny yourself a wondrous journey.

☐ **If I Don't Like It or Get It, It's Not Art; If I Don't Like It or Get It, It's Not Good Art**

This is really a set of four beliefs:

- If I don't like it, it's not art.
- If I don't get it, it's not art.
- If I don't like it, it's not good art.
- If I don't get it, it's not good art.

While working at The Fort Worth Art Museum, I was surprised by the number of disparaging remarks I overheard as the guests walked through the galleries. "That's ridiculous." "That can't be art." "I don't get it." "What makes that art?"

I observed that, understandably, those people had little tolerance for what they didn't comprehend or find appealing. As a result, they expressed their frustration by declaring that the art they were viewing was either not art or not good art.

I have come to realize that those people at the museum were not isolated cases but rather, if you will, the norm. Over time, I have heard the same sentiments expressed over and over again.

I have compassion for the people in this predicament. It's difficult to remain open-minded in the presence of that which we don't understand or like.

But here's where I draw the line. Not liking or not getting a work of art simply means that you don't like it or get it. It has no relationship to its validity or quality. In fact, that's all the more reason to explore it and discover some new things about it.

When you encounter art that you find difficult or unappealing, I encourage you to give it the benefit of the doubt and dive into it.

☐ Art Should Be Judged by Its Apparent Degree of Technical Difficulty

In our goal-oriented, competitive society, we are inundated with opportunities to judge performance by its degree of technical difficulty. Competitive gymnastics, figure skating and ballroom dancing are all cases in point. It seems we have come to believe that the more difficult anything is to execute, the better it is. No wonder this approach gets extended to art.

But art is not intended to be judged in this way. When artists are in the process of creating works of art, they aren't thinking about how difficult something is to produce but rather how best to express themselves creatively.

The question to ask yourself is not how difficult a work of art was to produce, but whether it touches your emotions, stimulates your senses and expands your intellect. Art is meant to be experienced, not graded!

☐ The Longer a Work of Art Took to Produce, the Better It Is and the More Money It's Worth

Let's debunk this Counterproductive Belief in one fell swoop.

There's a legend (attributed variously to James McNeill Whistler, Pablo Picasso and Jackson Pollock) in which an artist, when asked how long a particular painting took to produce, quipped, "All my life."

Every work of art produced by an artist, regardless of how long it took to create, is a product of that artist's entire life experience—including all of their education and training, all the ways they developed and grew as an artist and all of their joys and disappointments.

The length of time any particular work of art took to produce is entirely beside the point.

☐ Art Should Be Pretty

You might be among those who tend to dismiss any and all art that doesn't look pretty to you. This Counterproductive Belief, like some of the others, began in childhood. I can almost hear the art teachers' voices cooing, "That's lovely, Steve!" Or, "Amy, can you make something pretty for us?"

There's no denying that pretty pictures can brighten a kitchen or make a business office homier. While neither profound nor thought-provoking, pretty pictures are pleasant to have around, not unlike background music. Run-of-the-mill still lifes, nondescript landscapes and predictable abstract designs all fall into a category known as "decorative art." They serve as decoration along with knickknacks and throw pillows.

However, art (serious art, fine art, art with a capital "A") is capable of so much more than just looking pretty. Think about this. Do you really spend much time delving into art that's only pretty or charming? Do you find it thought-provoking? Are your emotions stirred in its presence? All this and more are available through art!

"But," you may ask, "what about the pretty art in museums?" Yes, not only can art be pretty, but it's often stunningly beautiful. However, all the "pretty" works of art you find in art museums go beyond being merely pretty. In every case, they have broken new ground or possess masterful attributes such as the inspired use of color, light and shadow.

Liberate yourself from the belief that art should be pretty. Once you let go of this Counterproductive Belief, your art-viewing experience will gain a depth and richness that was previously unavailable.

☐ Art Must Be Lofty, Solemn and Serious

You may have noticed that the European aristocrats depicted in centuries-old portraits wear solemn expressions. That's due to the fact that those aristocrats didn't want to "lower themselves" to appear in any way similar to the peasants, whom they viewed as frivolous, grinning drunks. Furthermore, since art was limited to the purview of the rich, it was supposed to be lofty, not down to earth.

Today, there is concern among conservative art community that, if art standards become excessively relaxed, art will become an intellectually watered-down extension of the entertainment industry.

Modern Art abandoned these notions and I invite you to do the same. Great Modern Art embraces every conceivable variation of mood and expression.

☐ Art Is Not Supposed to Be Funny

Have you ever caught sight of a work of art in a gallery or museum and suppressed the urge to giggle? Or maybe you laughed outright. Did you wonder if the art was supposed to be funny?

If you've encountered art that tickled your funny bone, but you suspected your reaction was inappropriate, chances are you believe that art is not supposed to be funny.

You may be glad to learn that you were most likely wrong about being wrong! Not only are many works of art intentionally humorous, but examples of jesting in art date all the way back to ancient Greece.

Here's the bottom line: If a work of art strikes you as funny, feel free to enjoy a good laugh.

☐ Art Should Not Be about Politics or Social Issues

Nonsense! Some of the most powerful works of art are political in nature.

Perhaps the most famous painting ever created by Pablo Picasso is *Guernica*, through which he communicates outrage at the Nazi bombing of the Spanish city of Guernica. This painting is a blatantly political statement, and its validity has never been questioned.

The Guerilla Girls, an art organization of female activists, have made it their mission to cause positive change in the art world and society at large. From their website: "We wear gorilla masks in public and use facts, humor and outrageous visuals to expose gender and ethnic bias as well as corruption in politics, art, film and pop culture."

Judy Chicago, a famous feminist artist, created *The Dinner Party*, widely regarded as the first epic feminist artwork. This work functions as a symbolic history of influential women in civilization and is clearly political in nature.

Robert Indiana created the well-known and highly controversial *Golden Future of America* in which he quoted Benjamin Franklin: "In free governments, the rulers are the servants and the people their sovereigns."

To say that art should not be political or social in nature is tantamount to saying that art should not reflect real life.

I invite you to celebrate the difference these courageous and brilliant works of political art make in the world.

With these Counterproductive Beliefs out of the way, Modern Art becomes so much more available for you to enjoy!

CHAPTER 6   COUNTERPRODUCTIVE BELIEFS – PERSPECTIVES THAT INTERFERE

I have to admit that, before I went to art school, I approached art as if the point were to decide whether or not I liked it and to mentally assign some sort of grade to it. I had never considered any other way of approaching art, and no one had ever suggested to me that there was another way.

I discovered in my college art critiques that there is so much more to be gained from art than just drawing a conclusion about it. In our critiques, each of us would put our most recent works on display and the whole class would discuss them. We engaged with each piece, finding that the more time we spent with it, the more there was to see and consider. As other people made comments about what they observed and experienced, new aspects of the art opened up for me—aspects I might not have noticed otherwise. Works that I might have written off became quite intriguing when explored with an open mind.

The beliefs in this section share one thing in common. Each of them involves an approach to art that shuts the door on exploration. The following four Counterproductive Beliefs are the biggest door-shutting culprits.

☐ The Point of Looking at Art Is to Determine Whether or Not It's Any Good

As an artist, I have frequently been advised to leave the criticism to the critics and to just do my job, which is making art. I'd like to give you similar advice. Leave the criticism to the critics! Your job is simply to experience the art.

The belief, "The point is to determine whether or not the art is any good," is almost universal. It's a tall order to set aside the inclination to pass judgment long enough to absorb and explore the art open-mindedly.

By the way, it's not that people walk around saying that the point is to determine whether any given work of art is good or not—it's that, when looking at art, they automatically arrive at a verdict. "This is good." "This one isn't any good." Or, they spend their precious time speculating about whether or not the art is any good.

This approach comes at a tremendous cost. The time you could have spent exploring the art was wasted on drawing conclusions that, in the long run, provide little satisfaction.

Am I saying that you should completely avoid forming an opinion about which art is good and which isn't? No, I'm not. We all do that automatically. It's just that it's not the best opening move if you want to "get the goods" from the art. After all, once you have decided that a work of art is or isn't any good, how likely are you to continue to engage with that work of art? You have all but rendered yourself unable to explore the art with an open mind.

By shifting your orientation from one of opinion-forming to inquiry and exploration, you will quickly find out what all the fuss is about when it comes to Modern Art. In fact, inquiry and exploration are the "keys to the kingdom" when it comes to Modern Art.

I recommend that you reserve judgment until you have spent some time with the art and allowed it to work its magic on you.

☐ The Point of Looking at Art Is to Determine Whether or Not You Like It

It's unquestionable that it's in our nature as human beings to make judgments about what we like and don't like. However, whether or not you like a work of art is actually beside the point.

Once you've made a determination for or against, you're essentially done with the art. You've robbed yourself of the deep and varied experiences that the art could offer.

This belief has no redeeming qualities and I invite you to let go of it right now.

☐ You Have to Study for Years to Truly Be Able to Appreciate Modern Art

There is a school of thought that the way to get what art has to offer is through knowledge—knowledge about the artists, color theory, composition, art history, art processes—knowledge, knowledge, knowledge!

I certainly don't dispute the benefits of knowledge when it comes to an intellectual understanding of art. However, the rich, deep, knock-your-socks-off experience that I know is possible for you will not happen as a result of understanding. It will come as you allow your natural affinity for art to emerge by simply being with the art rather than analyzing it.

There are other versions of this Counterproductive Belief, such as, "You have to take art appreciation classes to truly appreciate Modern Art," or "You have to learn art history to be able to appreciate Modern Art." You are not alone if you have a belief akin to these.

Well, I am here to tell you that when you study, what you get is information. Studying art history is a great thing to do if you want to get the big picture of how art has evolved and transformed over time. It's interesting to find out, for example, how the Moorish invasion of Spain influenced Spanish architecture or how Picasso's work paved the way for more than one art movement.

But do you have to study for years to truly be able to appreciate Modern Art? Emphatically not. Information is not the entry point into the glorious experience that occurs when you are simply being with the art.

Not only is it unnecessary to study for years to be able to truly appreciate Modern Art, it's actually easier to get into that delicious zone when your mind is unencumbered by too much information!

☐ I Already Know What I Like and Don't Like; Why Not Leave Well Enough Alone?

At a recent family gathering, I shared that I was writing this book. The art lover in the clan, Aunt Gennie, asked, "I know what I like. What's there to write about?" I replied, "It's great that there's art you like. But, like any activity in life, the more you engage with it, the richer and more rewarding it becomes."

My husband, Otto, is a software developer and tends to be very cerebral. I look at art and become completely enveloped in the experience. He looks at the same art and thinks about its context in history and the artist's life story. When we share afterward about the art, he might tell me about the artist's family tree and that period in history, while I describe how the art affected me and its visual aspects like the color, shape, texture and form.

One time, he and I were visiting a Modern Art museum together. In one of the galleries was a multi-colored sculpture of welded scrap metal parts from bicycles and who-knows-what. Otto had a negative reaction to it and said, "That just looks like junk to me." Truth be told, it wasn't love at first sight for me, either. But my trained response is to spend some time with art that doesn't attract me at first.

So, rather than move on, I suggested we spend some time with the piece. That way, we could both get present to it. We walked around it and looked at it from different angles and talked about what we noticed. We discovered some very interesting visual aspects and became especially fascinated by the intricate ways the shapes interacted with one another. We were surprised to find out that the sculpture evoked childhood memories for both of us. A piece that, initially, neither of us found appealing became a rewarding shared adventure.

When you dare to engage with art that you don't like at first sight, unpredictable, delightful experiences await you.

ⁿ

I cannot overstate the value of releasing these particular Counterproductive Beliefs. The approach you take ultimately determines whether or not you will have the magical experience with Modern Art that I promise is possible.

CHAPTER 7   COUNTERPRODUCTIVE BELIEFS – STEREOTYPES ABOUT ARTISTS

For the most part, I think that artists are born, not made. Most of the artists I've ever known were aware that they were artists from a very young age. It isn't something we become; it's something we are.

I was an adopted only child with nary an artist of any kind in my adoptive clan. Yet, there I was as a toddler— head down, bent over paper and paints and tissue paper and art book pictures. I loved everything having to do with art.

I definitely didn't fit the mold of what was considered normal in my adoptive family. Although my parents went out of their way to nurture my artistic talent, they didn't seem to know how to relate to me. According to my mother, I had no common sense, wore my heart on my sleeve and was overly emotional. I would often overhear her on the phone with her friends, responding to some unknown comment they had made about me, "Oh, don't mind her. She's an artist."

Like many artists, I have earned my living at a myriad of professions. And yet, throughout it all, I never stopped creating art.

All of this serves as an entree into the topic at hand—Counterproductive Beliefs about artists.

In truth, I don't know the extent to which Counterproductive Beliefs about artists influence your experience of viewing an artists' work. No doubt, it varies from person to person. These beliefs may not get in your way at all, or they could engender a bias that stops you from delving further into work whose validity you might question anyway.

The point of this chapter is to distinguish some of the stereotypical beliefs about artists that could be interfering with your having a productive and stimulating art-viewing experience.

☐ Artists Are Entirely Right-Brained; They Are Not Strong Cognitive Thinkers

Artists epitomize creative (right-brained) thinking. That does not mean, however, that they are only right-brained. Au contraire! Artists tend to be intensely intelligent, exceptionally articulate and many of us are highly organized.

Obviously, the ability to think creatively is a must for artists. However, there are many aspects of art-making that involve physics, chemistry and engineering, all of which necessitate left-brained functions. For example, painting is one of the most straightforward mediums, and even it requires knowledge of color theory, composition, color mixing, paint and paint medium characteristics and so on.

The process of moving an artistic inspiration from conception to completion is often an undertaking of mammoth proportion. Not only does it demand that artists fully utilize their right-brain capacities, but they must often build partnerships, conduct research, coordinate multiple actions and communicate effectively with fabricators, other artists, vendors and gallerists. These all require the use of the left brain.

Many artists are employed as professors and are gifted teachers. In those roles, they demonstrate daily their ability to articulate art distinctions such that students are empowered to develop as artists. These professors are so well versed in art history that they can, without missing a beat, reference specific artists' work, art periods and styles as they guide their students' development. More evidence of the left brain at work.

For an artist to manage their own art career requires strong verbal and writing skills, organizational facility and a great deal of general business savvy. Artists are routinely called upon to write grant proposals, artists' statements and descriptions of their work—still more evidence of the left brain in action. And let us not forget about accounting.

In short, you can put this Counterproductive Belief to rest. I'm not sure how the belief, "Artists are entirely right-brained," originated, but I can tell you that it's not anywhere close to the truth.

☐ Artists Don't Work Hard

Artists tend to be viewed as free spirits. Creating art is often considered child's play, and art classes are all too frequently seen as strictly recreational and devoid of educational value. Such views reinforce the belief that artists don't work hard.

Let's get to the truth of the matter. If you were to watch an artist work for a week or even for a day, you would see that creating art is serious work. It requires intensive thinking and planning, often hard physical labor plus significant emotional investment. Some artists don't work from nine to five, but there's a good chance they're working feverishly on some idea that has captured their passion long after others have turned in for the night.

In a sense, artists are always working—incubating ideas, pondering technical solutions to problems, being present to everything in the environment that could ignite a new idea. When artists look at other artists' work, they are not only immersed in the art, they're also working—making themselves available for the almost inevitable moments of inspiration.

Creating works of art means taking risks, treading new territory and finding fresh ways of expressing ideas.

Artists don't work hard? Are you kidding me?

☐ Artists Are Weird

In case you have any doubt, "weird" is not used in the complimentary sense here. I'm referring to the labeling that is derogatory and dismissive.

There are so many angles from which to address this Counterproductive Belief.

To begin to derail this notion, it can be said that anything unfamiliar or unusual might seem "weird." But that has more to do with the conventions in any community than it does with the person or group that's being called "weird." Said another way, what's weird to one person is completely normal to another.

On a more practical level, let's look at the fact that a lot of artists dress, talk and act in ways that are unlike the majority of any given society. Artists' living spaces are also often very unusual. All of these are outward expressions of creativity. Artists are creative and they apply this creativity to every area in their lives.

On a personal note, I am consciously creative about my physical appearance and the design of my home. I have been told that I'm weird, but, in all honesty, to me it's weird that not everyone loves to apply their creativity and individuality to their look and to their living spaces.

All that said, not all artists fit the stereotype of being unconventional or "weird." I've known many artists who dress, act and live in very conventional ways.

I suspect that believing artists are weird is likely to give you an "out" when looking at art that you find challenging. By this I mean that you might dismiss a challenging work of art by reminding yourself that artists are weird, so why bother to engage with "weird art?"

So, I invite you to either let go of this Counterproductive Belief or reinterpret "weird" as a good thing.

☐ Artists Are Flighty and Unreliable

You may have inherited this belief from others or had personal interactions that prompted you to conclude that artists are flighty and unreliable.

Here's what I have to say about that. While it's true that there are flighty, unreliable artists in the world, it's also true that there's an abundance of steady, dependable artists. I have known many artists personally and professionally, and most of us take our commitments quite seriously and pride ourselves on being responsible. The mischief occurs when we lump all artists together as if they were all just alike.

The bottom line here is that artists run the full gamut—from being rock-solid with their commitments to being air-heads—just like people of all professions!

☐ Artists Are Temperamental

I have had the great fortune to interact with some of the most influential artists of our time. When I worked at the Modern Art museum in Fort Worth, I loved assisting the installation crew, which meant working directly with famous artists. Almost all of them were friendly and gracious.

In looking back over my career, I can honestly say I've interacted with only four or five artists in total who seemed decidedly temperamental. They were the rare exceptions.

While I haven't had the chance to observe every artist in every possible situation, I feel confident in saying that this Counterproductive Belief is simply hogwash!

If any of these Counterproductive Beliefs about artists were keeping you from fully appreciating Modern Art, letting go of them is guaranteed to leave you with more freedom to simply enjoy the art.

CHAPTER 8   COUNTERPRODUCTIVE BELIEFS – THE NOT-SO-FRIENDLY ART WORLD

I'd like to talk about the term "art world." It's a term that is used often and loosely. If I'm in a conversation with a group of people and someone asks, "What's happening in the art world?" no one questions the meaning of the term. Obviously, it's not a physical world, nor is there some actual location called the "art world." It's just a concept.

Wikipedia describes the art world in this way: "The art world comprises everyone involved in producing, commissioning, presenting, preserving, promoting, chronicling, criticizing, and selling fine art." It goes on to state, "'Art world' is a wider term than art market, though the art market is a large part of it."'

The key word in the Wikipedia definition is "fine." The term "art world" refers to all the goings-on in the world having to do with significant or important art—the art shown in museums and discussed in magazines like ARTnews and Art Forum.

You can compare the art world to the fashion industry. If you have a friend who makes tie-dye tee shirts and sells them online, you probably wouldn't think of that person as part of the fashion industry. Similarly, if your neighbor paints picturesque sailboats on wood, although technically that person is producing artwork, their work wouldn't be considered part of the art world.

At any rate, you now have at least some sense of what is meant by the term "art world." This should assist you in looking at and dismantling the Counterproductive Beliefs about the art world that could be stopping you from enjoying art.

☐ The Art World Is Intentionally Exclusive

Art has a long history of being the domain of the ruling class. To this day, that rarefied echelon of the art market wherein art is auctioned off for millions of dollars obviously remains the realm of the rich.

Is the art world intentionally exclusive? Unfortunately, I have to say yes, in some respects. For example, the high-end art market is quite intentionally exclusive. After all, what cachet would it give the uber-rich to collect the most "important" art if everyone could do it?

The very fact that the art you see in museums is ultra-expensive adds fuel to the argument that the art market is intentionally exclusive. In fact, if it weren't for museums, we ordinary folk would be hard-pressed to see the extensive collections of world-class art that they exhibit!

I think it's important to understand that artists create their work to share with everyone—not just certain people. And artists are the most essential part of the art world, wouldn't you say?

Let's get back to whether the art world is intentionally exclusive. It seems that art museums have been exclusive by tradition and by default, but not by intention. In fact, many major art museums in the United States are awake to the fact that people find museums stuffy and intimidating. They are going to considerable lengths to become more friendly, interesting and accessible to the public at large. They are instituting interactive programs that educate and engage children and adults alike in participating with art—especially Modern and Contemporary Art.

All that said, even if you find the art world exclusive, much of the art you'll find in museums and fine art galleries promises to be more than worth your time. I invite you to dive into every art experience with an attitude of curiosity. You might discover yourself in a fun, friendly atmosphere, and if not, there's always the amazing art to enjoy!

☐ The Art World Is Snobbish

Like any stereotype, there is some basis in reality for this Counterproductive Belief. You might find certain gallerists and museum staff less than approachable and, yes, snobbish.

I could hardly believe my eyes when I discovered that the Merriam-Webster dictionary featured this sample sentence for the word, "snob." "The snobs at the museum fund-raiser turned their little noses up at us because we weren't wearing designer outfits." This speaks to the universality of this belief!

But is it true that everyone in the art world is snobbish? No. Many of them are quite friendly. Others could be shy, introverted, insecure, busy, upset or distracted. Perhaps if we were to interact with the same people on a different day, they might be outgoing and friendly.

If you ever find yourself intimidated by the attitude of gallery staff, let me remind you that art galleries are simply retail stores that sell art. When you walk into any gallery, think of yourself as a valued customer and potential buyer. (By the way, consider the possibility that, if the staff doesn't seem friendly, they might be giving you space to enjoy the art in peace.)

When you hold fast to the belief that the art world is snobbish, every time you walk into any art venue, you will expect to be treated with condescension or ignored altogether. This is a recipe for anything but a great day viewing art!

If, on the other hand, you are willing to loosen your grip on the belief that the art world is snobbish, at least three things could happen: 1) You might find yourself more relaxed and open whenever you're in a museum or gallery; 2) You could be present to the art rather than your discomfort; and 3) You might have some great conversations with the people there!

☐ The Art World Is Pretentious

Just like the first two Counterproductive Beliefs in this chapter, there is some truth to this one. So, rather than debunk it, I will explore it, present some ways to re-think it, and, I hope, leave you with more freedom to be yourself in any art milieu.

Most art exhibition spaces have a veneer of importance and austerity so as to elevate the art and its insiders to a higher level of importance than they might otherwise have. Unfortunately, many of us find this type of atmosphere uncomfortable.

In truth, art could be presented in a variety of ways with no loss of power. Do the guests really need to be dressed in expensive fashions? Is it necessary for the staff to be so reserved? Could people speak above a whisper?

If you're someone who finds this type of atmosphere unpleasant, does that mean that your only choices are to stay away or suffer through it? Not at all.

There's an alternative that doesn't necessitate a change in circumstances. It involves making a simple mental adjustment. Consider this—there is more than one way to interpret any situation or human behavior. For example, you could think of a child as mischievous or spirited; you could look at someone as frugal or miserly; similarly, you could interpret gallery staff as standoffish or respectful of your space.

What are some ways that you could re-interpret "pretentious?" One re-interpretation that works for me is to suppose that the people at the events are all eager to have meaningful conversations, but are too shy or awkward to initiate them. You could be the initiator. That's what I do!

The trick to creating an authentic shift is to invent a new interpretation that not only empowers you but also takes the indisputable facts into account. In other words, you're not denying what's before your eyes—you're just looking at it a different way.

So, rather than be intimidated or uncomfortable at that art gala, why not approach the event with curiosity and a sense of adventure? That way, you could enjoy the art and the whole experience.

This chapter revealed some of the ways that Counterproductive Beliefs about the art world might be putting a damper on your ability to enjoy art. Rather than debunk these beliefs, I have pointed out ways to interact with the art world from a fresh perspective—one that leaves you free to experience the true magic of Modern Art.

CHAPTER 9   COUNTERPRODUCTIVE BELIEFS – MODERN ART, THE CRUX OF THE MATTER

Appreciating Modern Art is something I grew into. I shared with you earlier that when I was twelve and first saw that fantastic Van Gogh exhibit, the world of Modern Art opened up for me. It wasn't as if a thunderbolt struck me and I suddenly loved all Modern Art. It was a gradual process, with the boundaries moving further and further out until I found myself enthusiastically embracing the most outrageously innovative art you can imagine!

So, here we are at the chapter that tackles the final category of Counterproductive Beliefs—those specific to Modern Art. It wouldn't be possible to debunk these beliefs had you not done the work you've done up to this point.

The first of these beliefs is a doozie—and it's one that runs rampant among those not yet on board with Modern Art.

☐ Modern Art Is a Sham

The Counterproductive Belief, "Modern Art is a sham," is a blanket disavowal of the validity of all Modern Art. It's a deal-breaker; it precludes any possibility of a positive relationship to Modern Art.

I think a leap of faith is required here. You have declared yourself willing to be open to Modern Art, and this is the time to draw upon that willingness. You may not yet feel able to put this belief to rest, but I'll bet you can put it aside long enough to test it out for yourself.

Appreciating art is all about experiencing it. You won't know for sure that Modern Art delivers the goods until you experience it for yourself.

Modern Art will open up to you as you open up to it. The more you open up, the more you will get from it.

☐ Modern Art Is Intentionally Obscure

There is nothing worse than optimistically approaching works of art and coming away feeling baffled or even stupid. When this happens, it's easy to suspect that the art was intended to leave us feeling that way.

I would be remiss not to acknowledge that, in rare cases, there are artists who have created works that are intentionally obscure. These artworks are meant to appear as if they contain some esoteric references or symbols that only the most savvy would grasp. Fortunately, you are unlikely to encounter these in a museum setting.

The fact is that the vast majority of artists do not set out to stump their audiences or create work that is intentionally obscure. On the contrary. Artists are compelled to express themselves authentically. They want nothing more than to share their expression with the world. Intending their art to be obscure is the furthest thing from their minds.

I hope that from now on, believing Modern Art to be intentionally obscure will be the furthest thing from your mind, as well!

☐ My Five-Year-Old Could Do That

I've overheard this belief a million times from the mouths of museum-goers. The smart-alecky response to this one is, "Go home and let your five-year-old give it a shot." If you were to take me up on this, you would quickly see that producing such a work is well beyond your five-year-old's abilities.

The simple truth is, just because a work of art looks as if anyone could do it doesn't mean that anyone could. Just like great dancers and musicians, great artists make what they do look easy. That's because they're extremely good at it.

Don't let it throw you if a work of art appears to have been a piece of cake to make. Take the time and trouble to explore those deceptively simple but often elegant, bold and energetic works of Modern Art.

Congratulations! You have now completed the process of unveiling and dispelling the Counterproductive Beliefs that have been standing between you and your natural affinity for Modern Art.

You are well on your way toward having the magic of Modern Art in your life!

Art evokes the mystery without which the world would not exist.

— René Magritte

PART THREE

Seeing Modern Art through New Eyes

CHAPTER 10   CHANGING GEARS – INVENTING A NEW CONTEXT FOR MODERN ART

Up to this point, you have:

- declared yourself open to all that Modern Art has to offer;
- learned about Counterproductive Beliefs and their role in prohibiting you from fully appreciating Modern Art; and
- released the specific Counterproductive Beliefs that applied to you.

You should be experiencing a sense of freedom, like an openness, that you didn't have before. Now we can address the notion of context as it applies to your relationship to Modern Art.

My Context for Modern Art

I knew I was an artist as far back as I can remember. As an only child of very protective parents, I spent a lot of time sequestered inside our house. This was not a problem for me since I was perfectly happy entertaining myself by painting, drawing and creating all manner of art projects. Thus arose my initial context for art, which was "art is fun."

When I was introduced to Modern Art at age 11, my context, "art is fun," automatically extended to include Modern Art. Of course, my relationship with Modern Art has deepened and matured over the years, but the context, "art is fun," still remains to this day and has allowed me to bring enjoyment and satisfaction to all things art.

Even when I encounter a work of art that strikes me as hideously ugly or otherwise unpleasant, often as not, I spend time with it, explore it, and inquire into what makes it seem so unappealing to me. When I encounter a work of art that's sad or disturbing, I let myself be present to it and to the reactions I'm having. Even upsetting or somber art is an enjoyable experience for me—enjoyable in that it engages me and enriches my experience of living. All thanks to my context, "art is fun."

Your Context for Modern Art

One of my most influential teachers taught me years ago that context is decisive. By that, he meant that the context determines what's possible and what's not possible in any given area of life.

Although you may not be aware of it, you already have a context for Modern Art. It may or may not be an empowering one. For example, if your context for Modern Art has been, "Modern Art is a sham," imagine how little is possible in terms of enjoying it. In fact, with that context, there's no chance for Modern Art to seem like anything but a sham to you.

It is not essential to identify your current context, but if you want to do that, that's totally fine. The point of this chapter is for you to create a context that supports your desire to get the goodies from Modern Art.

A Context I Created

After completing my undergraduate art degree, I found my way to a full-time career creating commissioned one-of-a-kind ceramic pieces. A Dallas art dealer heard about my work and sought me out. He became my art representative and, not long after that, my husband. We were immersed in the Dallas art scene. We also traveled the country interacting with artists from many art communities.

As you can imagine, I had the opportunity to engage in numerous discussions with artists about art. I noticed a qualitative difference in the conversations with those artists who held a master's degree in art compared with those who didn't. Observations made by the artists with master's degrees often included concepts and even terminology that went right over my head. This piqued my interest in going back to school. Getting my master's degree had long been a dream of mine anyway; discovering that there were distinctions in art that I had yet to learn provided the final impetus.

So, I invented the context, "becoming privy to the finer distinctions of art," for my years in graduate school. And guess what? Gaining those distinctions was one of the highlights of my graduate art school experience.

Thanks to that context, I was avidly engaged in the critique discussions. I listened eagerly to all of the conversations on art theory. Had I created a different context for graduate school, such as "acquiring the credentials to become a college professor," I have no doubt that my time in graduate school would have seemed quite different. I would still have gained new distinctions, but I doubt that that particular aspect of my school experience would have stood out for me so prominently.

To this day, I'm grateful for the impact of that context on my life. Not only did it enhance the time I spent in graduate school, but it gave me an even deeper appreciation for Modern Art.

Inventing Your New Context for Modern Art

The context you are about to create for your relationship with Modern Art has the potential to be as powerful for you as mine has been for me.

It is important that your new context be an authentic expression for you—one that inspires and empowers you. The words you choose should feel right to you because this new context will set the tone for your relationship with Modern Art.

So, how do you invent a new context? I have found that it's useful to begin by brainstorming, using key questions as prompts. Here are two questions that I think will point you in the right direction.

1. What do you want your time with Modern Art to be about?
2. What do you want from your experience with Modern Art?

For example, you might want your time with Modern Art to be about exploration or stimulation. Or maybe you just want it to be fun. Mind-expansion, surprise or amazement might fit the bill for you. What about awe, wonder, curiosity or mystery? Maybe you're seeking a disruption to your everyday thinking or a respite from the daily grind.

The possible contexts for Modern Art are endless!

I suggest you take some time to come up with your own word, phrase or sentence that best captures what you want from Modern Art. If any of the previously mentioned suggestions is a good fit for you, feel free to use it. Otherwise, keep looking for the word or words that resonate with you.

Since you are creating a context that inspires and excites you, I encourage you to take all the time you need. What you're looking for here is a context that gives you a sense of anticipation about your future visits to Modern Art exhibits.

Creating a powerful context for your relationship with Modern Art is a huge leap forward. In the next chapter, you will be introduced to The Magic of Modern Art Tour, which will give you access to Modern Art on a whole new level!

The time has come for you to see Modern Art through new eyes. I have just the thing to ensure your success—The Magic of Modern Art Tour! The Magic of Modern Art Tour (originally the Robyn Jamison Art Tour) began as an experiment. I wanted to find out if the process I had invented would bring about a breakthrough for people who were not in touch with their natural affinity for Modern Art.

As I share throughout this book, I believe that the key to unlocking the magic of Modern Art is to immerse oneself in the art and truly experience it. Much to my delight, every single person who has taken my tour has confirmed that they had a breakthrough in their appreciation for Modern Art.

The Magic of Modern Art Tour is designed to guide you through a process of discovery. You can expect to make three significant discoveries when you take the tour.

The first discovery is that you have the ability to be fully present with the art. This discovery happens on the job, so to speak—it's an experiential discovery.

The second discovery is that being with the art is distinct from analyzing or judging it. Curiosity and wonder are all you need.

The third discovery is that, when you do have that experience of being with the art, all the great stuff that seasoned art lovers say happens to them, also happens to you. The closest I can come to describing this in words is a sense of awe and a welling up of joy.

How to Take Yourself on The Magic of Modern Art Tour

To prepare, I highly recommend that you have with you the instructions for the Magic of Modern Tour. They're available in multiple locations. This chapter walks you through the long version with lots of explanations. The graphic in Appendix A is an abbreviated step-by-step instruction guide. You can also get the instruction guide via this link: www.MagicOfModernArt.com/OnTheGo or with the QR code at the end of the Afterword.

Here's how to begin. Select a Modern Art exhibit to visit. I recommend that you choose a Modern Art exhibit in a museum, if possible. If there's no museum in your vicinity, a gallery will do nicely. It is, however, vital that you attend an exhibit in person; art reproductions are not good substitutes and will not yield similar results.

I suggest that you go with at least one other person. This will give you the opportunity to debrief your experience, make new discoveries, express new insights and solidify all of that in a dialogue.

As soon as you arrive at the museum or gallery, take a moment to do two things. Remind yourself that you've declared yourself open to all that Modern Art has to offer, and re-presence the new context you created.

So, there you are at the exhibit. The next part of the process is best done in solitude. Find a peaceful spot and take a few deep breaths.

Then, spend a few minutes getting an overall impression of the entire show. If it's in one open gallery space, look around the room. If the exhibit extends into more than one room, walk through without stopping in front of any one work of art.

Once you've scanned the whole exhibit, identify a work of art toward which you have an immediate negative reaction. Yes, a negative reaction. That's the first work of art that you will focus on. You will be spending some time looking at and absorbing this work of art that you would normally be inclined to avoid. Plan to spend at least 15 minutes focused on this work. Half an hour is ideal.

Now, approach the art, stop at a comfortable distance and just take it in. Don't rush. Depending on the size and placement of the piece, you may want to move around slowly and look at it from a variety of distances and angles. Notice how it looks from several vantage points and whether your responses to it change as you move.

Then, find a spot that allows you to see the piece comfortably. If it's large, get back far enough to be able to see the whole thing. If it's small, come in closer. Stand (or sit) silently before it. Just be with the art, almost as if you were meditating, but remaining focused on the work in front of you. It's okay to move around from time to time or stay in one spot. The important thing is that you immerse yourself in the art for the time allotted.

As you look at the piece, observe your thoughts; let them roam freely. Just notice them. Try not to argue with the thoughts or attempt to change them. Avoid believing or agreeing with your thoughts. It may feel strange just to notice your thoughts and not do anything with them—and that's okay.

You might ask yourself, "Are these thoughts familiar? Do they reflect some of my old Counterproductive Beliefs?" Don't worry if the same thoughts you've had before come up. After all, thoughts happen automatically. If some of those old familiar thoughts pop up, do you notice that they don't have the same grip on you?

You also may find yourself drawing a conclusion about the work of art you're viewing. That's not a problem, but don't believe that conclusion or stop being with the piece before the designated time is up.

Trust that the effort you have put in so far has made a difference. You have debunked your Counterproductive Beliefs and created a new context. The difference between the past and present is this: now you know that you no longer have to believe those beliefs, even if they do come up. You could consider them of no more consequence than a staticky radio station playing in the background.

Meanwhile, begin to notice any emotions that come up. What emotions are they? Are they shifting from one to another or remaining the same? Do not try to change or control them. No matter what emotions you experience—anger, sadness, joy, fear—they are all fine. Just observe them and let them be.

You may also become aware of bodily sensations. Are they pleasant or unpleasant? Just as with the thoughts and emotions, there's nothing to do about the sensations other than to observe them and allow them to be there.

Consider any reactions that you have to the artwork as an opportunity for you to learn or recognize something about yourself. For example, if you find yourself feeling offended or irritated, you can ask yourself, 'What is it about me that would have me respond that way? What button did it push in me?" Art is meant to be provocative, and it's often very growth-inducing.

When the designated time is over, ask yourself whether this work of art seems any different to you now after having spent some time with it. If so, in what way is it different? What do you now see about it that you didn't see when you first encountered it? What are you experiencing after having spent time with it?

Whatever your experience is, it is absolutely valid and, in fact, perfect. This even includes the case where you're not aware of having discovered or learned anything.

If you went to the exhibit with at least one other person, I encourage you to share your experiences with each other.

Once you have debriefed your experience, I suggest you select another work of art. This time, it can be one that you like immediately or another toward which you have an adverse reaction. Either way, repeat the process.

If you're feeling a bit spent, simply move on through the exhibit at a leisurely pace, maintaining both your solitude and your silence. When you feel "full," it's time to leave the exhibit. Taking in art uses considerable energy!

I encourage you to give yourself the Magic of Modern Art Tour every time you attend a Modern Art exhibit. Feel free to modify it as you become more at home with the process.

Your sense of connection to Modern Art and the magic it delivers will continue to unfold over time. I wish you many magical hours in the presence of Modern Art!

CHAPTER 12   ALTERNATE APPROACHES – OTHER MODERN ART TOURS TO TRY

Once you have begun to experience the wonders of Modern Art through The Magic of Modern Art Tour, you might also enjoy exploring Modern Art in other ways. This chapter describes four different approaches which I consider to be particularly effective for getting into Modern Art.

Do This Every Time

Whenever you find yourself in a Modern Art museum or gallery, it's helpful to begin by taking a few deep breaths and getting settled before moving on to the art. Since the key to loving Modern Art is the ability to experience it, being in a contemplative "head-space" will serve you well.

Describing What You See and What You Experience

This approach is especially useful when you're looking at art that's unfamiliar to you or when it doesn't work for you to be with any one piece for an extended period of time. This approach can be fun, almost like playing twenty questions. You are being introduced to the art in a way that's similar to how you might make a new acquaintance. I like this method because it gives you a sense of clarity and groundedness.

Here are some questions to use as prompts for your inquiry. (These questions are included on the Magic of Modern Art website, www.MagicOfModernArt.com/OnTheGo, as well as in Appendix B.)

Is it a two-dimensional or three-dimensional work?
What shape or shapes comprise it?
Are the shapes geometric or organic?

Does this work of art resemble something recognizable?
If so, how realistic does it look?
If it doesn't resemble anything recognizable, describe the way it looks.

What is the scale of this piece?

Does it represent something from life?

If so, is it life-size, larger-than-life or smaller than the thing it represents?

Does it make you want to look at it from far back or up close?

What is the medium?

Oil on canvas?

Welded metal?

Carved wood?

Mixed media?

Other?

What is the color scheme?

Is there a broad range of colors or a limited palette?

Are the colors mostly light or dark, brilliant or subdued?

Is there a lot of contrast?

Do the colors overlap?

How is the paint (or other material) applied?

Does it appear to have been applied quickly or slowly?

Is it thick, roughly textured or smooth?

Is the finish shiny or matte?

Are there visible brushstrokes?

Are the brushstrokes translucent or opaque?

What path do your eyes follow as you look at the piece?

Do your eyes move quickly or slowly?

Does your gaze want to move outside the piece or does it stay within its boundaries?

Do your eyes keep returning to a focal point?

What do you observe about the composition (design) of this piece?

Is it symmetrical or asymmetrical?

Does it have a feeling of balance or imbalance?

Are the shapes or lines confined within the overall piece or do they go outside the borders?

Does it look busy or minimalistic?

What is the overall feeling or mood of the piece?

Does it feel settled or unsettled?

Does it seem orderly or chaotic?

How do you feel as you explore this work of art?

What do you think the piece is about or is intended to communicate?

Does it seem to be expressing a certain point of view?

When you look at it, does it remind you of anything?

How are you left after interacting with this piece?

Has it brought up any memories?

Do you find yourself in a different mood?

What do you notice about your energy level?

Are you left thinking about the piece itself?

Do you feel like your creativity has been stimulated?

Once you have considered these questions, I encourage you to spend at least a few more minutes just being with the piece before moving on to the next one.

Even though this approach is less time-consuming than The Magic of Modern Art Tour, it does take some time. I do not recommend that you do this with every single piece in the exhibit unless it's a very small show or you have all day.

Entering the Artist's World

In the "Describing What You See and What You Experience" tour, the aim is to let the art into your consciousness and discover how it affects you.

In the "Entering the Artist's World" approach, the objective is to get a sense of what it might have been like for the artist to create their works of art. You will consider what their mood might have been and why the artist made the choices they made while creating the art. Another way of saying all this is that you are going to notice as much as you can about the work of art and imagine the how and why of it from the artist's perspective.

Since the inception of Modern Art, artists have enjoyed more and more freedom to use any medium in any way in order to express anything and everything. Exploring what's behind all of their choices can be both intriguing and enlightening. Each and every one of their choices reveals something about the artists and the art.

For this particular approach, it's helpful to first look around the entire exhibit to determine whether the artist created all the work in the show during one artistic phase or whether the show represents a cross-section of periods of the artist's career.

In the following paragraphs, I provide a broad overview of this approach, plus some questions to support your exploration. There is also an expanded set of questions at www.MagicOfModernArt.com/OnTheGo and in the diagram in Appendix B.

As I mentioned before, the decisions that artists make are quite revealing, beginning with their choices of mediums and methodologies.

When I was in undergraduate school, I studied Art Education, which required me to take classes in an extensive range of mediums. I quickly discovered which ones did and did not suit my personality. For example, even though I loved coming up with designs for fine metalwork, I found the hours of sanding and finishing to be excruciatingly tedious. On the other hand, the immediacy of drawing and painting fit me perfectly.

In looking at what it was like for an artist to create any given work of art, there are certain types of questions that, when answered, will provide you with insight.

For example, a question to consider is, "What steps were involved in producing this work of art, all the way from conception to completion?"

Along the same lines, "How much time does it appear to have taken to create the piece?" If, for example, it was cast in bronze, it involved a long, labor-intensive process and probably required assistance from other people. If it's a watercolor painting with just a few quickly brushed strokes of color, it may have been completed in minutes or even just seconds.

What do you think the difference in experience is for an artist to work on something for many days as opposed to going from start to finish in a short period of time? What does it tell you about the type of person the artist is likely to be in each case?

All these considerations can make for an engaging inquiry during your art visit.

To engage you even more, here is a compilation of my favorite questions to guide you through this process. (You might notice it includes the prompts I mentioned above.)

What did it take for the artist to bring this work from conception to completion?
>   What might have been involved in producing this work of art?

What is the medium?
>   Did the artist use the medium in a unique or unusual way?
>   Why might the artist have chosen this medium?

If the work is very large, how might the artist have executed it?
>   How did the artist position him or herself to work on it?
>   Why might the artist have chosen to work on such a large scale?
>   What could the artist have wanted to convey by working so large?

If the work is very small, how might the artist have executed it?
>How did the artist position him or herself to work on it?
>Why might the artist have chosen to work on such a small scale?
>What could the artist have wanted to convey by working so small?

How much time does it appear to have taken to create this piece?
>How might the length of time it took to complete the piece have impacted the artist's experience of creating it?
>What does it tell you about the type of person the artist is likely to be?

What is the texture of the surface?
>How and with what tools might the artist have created that texture?
>How might the artist have moved his or her hand, arm or whole body to produce such a texture?
>What could the artist have intended to express through this choice of texture?
>If there is more than one texture, ask yourself these same questions for each one.

What kinds of colors are used for this piece?
>What could the choice of color scheme tell us about the artist or the artist's state of mind?
>Do the color choices seem to express a particular mood?
>What might all these color choices indicate about how the artist was feeling?

If the work looks particularly complex or particularly simple, how did the artist get it to look that way?
>What might this quality communicate about the artist's personality or nature?
>What could the artist have wanted to convey by choosing a simple or complex composition?

What is the overall feeling or mood of the piece?
>What might the artist have been feeling while creating this work of art?

What other questions or explorations come to mind about the artist's experience in creating this work of art?

This approach can leave you with the feeling that you know the artist and give you a deeper appreciation for their work.

If you happen to be at an art opening, you might even have the opportunity to meet the artist and ask them questions about their work. After all, what better way to get into the world of the artist than to actually speak with the artist?

Familiarizing Yourself with the Artist

My husband enjoys going with me to see Modern Art exhibits. While I'm soaking in the experience of being with the art, he's researching the artists' lives.

Knowing about artists' lives can certainly add another dimension to your appreciation for their art. A case in point is Frida Kahlo, whose work is a direct expression of the horrific injury she suffered at age 18, leaving her in tremendous pain for the rest of her life. Another is Jean-Michel Basquiat, who grew up with extraordinary educational opportunities against the backdrop of his mother's mental illness and family instability. Basquiat's work reflects his street-graffiti days and his street-wise ways.

It can also be fascinating to explore the full range of an artist's work. Often, famous artists are known for a particular subset of their entire body of work. Andy Warhol is most famous for his soup cans and portraits of celebrities. You may not be aware that he created a significant amount of artwork that features religious iconography, thanks to his Catholic roots.

Damien Hirst is best known for his controversial works which feature animal carcasses preserved in steel and glass tanks filled with formaldehyde. He later made a radical switch to colorful paintings including such subjects as rainbows, hearts and flowers!

It's so easy to look at works of art and forget that they were made by human beings whose artwork is an expression of their individuality. Learning about their lives is a wonderful way to enrich your experience of their art.

Taking Advantage of Museum Resources

Perhaps you've taken docent or audio tours or read the pamphlets or wall-text that often accompany art exhibits in museums. These are tried-and-true ways to gain information about the art.

They are not my favorite methods, however, when it comes to Modern Art because I think they take the juiciest part of the experience away—its mystery. I firmly believe that Modern Art is meant to be explored, not explained.

That said, if you are at an exhibit that you can't relate to at all, the information provided by the museum can provide guidance.

Anything that motivates you and enhances the time you spend participating with Modern Art is worthwhile.

If you opt to take a tour or do some reading, I recommend that you spend some time with the art first. That way, your initial experience of the art will be fresh, not influenced by what you hear or read.

Above all, remember: there's not a fixed, correct interpretation when it comes to Modern Art, and your experience, even if it's totally opposite of what you read or hear, is perfectly valid. It's your experience. How can experience be wrong?

So there you have it—a few additional ways to get into Modern Art. As you become a seasoned Modern Art viewer, you will undoubtedly create variations of these and even invent entirely new approaches.

CHAPTER 13   INTERVIEWS WITH THE PROS – THEIR PERSPECTIVES ON MODERN ART

One of the things I enjoy most about interacting with other artists and art professionals is learning about their diverse perspectives on Modern Art. We all share a love for Modern Art, but what we love about it and how we love it vary considerably.

When I was in the planning stages of writing this book, I thought it would be extremely valuable for you to get some perspectives other than my own. I particularly wanted to dispel the myth that there is only one correct way to look at Modern Art.

With that in mind, I conducted a series of interviews with seventeen art professionals, including artists, academics, gallerists, a director of a non-profit art center and an art school director. Interviewing them was a delightful, fascinating and inspiring experience for me. To say that it was difficult to choose which of their brilliant, enlightening quotes to include in this book is an understatement.

The artists I interviewed produce unique and extraordinary works of art. Examples of their work follow the interview quotes. You can find a brief bio of each interviewee in Appendix C.

Enjoy!

1) What advice do you have for anyone who wants to get the most out of viewing Modern Art?

The responses to this question were so insightful and diverse that I couldn't resist including all of them. Hint: they are all worth reading!

Jonathan Tung: Go into it with your own eyes. Don't look at it colored through somebody else's interpretation.

Look at the piece first. Read the tag last. Once you read that tag, that work is already in a box, so your viewing is going to be colored by that information. Trust your own instinct.

Becky Hendrick: Don't pass judgment. Keep your likes and dislikes separate from the experience.

You can respond personally but just then say, "Wait a minute. There's a reason why it's in a museum." It wasn't chosen frivolously.

When you pass judgment, you're closing the door.

Sally Weber: Imagine going to a new restaurant. You might never have had that kind of cuisine before. You're experiencing something different, and you don't have an opinion yet. Well, what's the experience of tasting it like? You don't have to eat all of it. You don't have to come back to that restaurant. But at least experience it for what it is.

Vincent Falsetta: Let go of preconceptions of what art should be. Let go of "knowing" what characteristics it has to have in order to be called good art. Let go of descriptions of good or bad and just try to experience the work.

Look at the work. Look at the glare. Look at what is reflective and what is matte. Look at how far apart things are from one another. Look at the patterns.

Aloma Marquis: Give yourself the room to dive in and expect to have some fun with it. Contemporary/Modern Art actually demands that you be a participant—notice I didn't say "viewer?" "Viewer" is passive. With realistic work, you don't have to do a lot because the information is given to you, so you're pretty much a passive receiver. With Contemporary Art, you've got to have some skin in the game. So you're going to bring your intelligence.

Joshua Kight: Like a really good poem, there is no bottom to it and there is no solution. It's not a math problem. The longer you spend with it, the more it disgorges its mysteries, but if it's a really great work of art, you can live with it for a lifetime.

Bob Adams: I would say, don't look for meaning. Just let the painting tell you what its meaning is. But I'm not saying it's in words. It can just be a visual impression.

That's what I love about art—art doesn't give you a little note at the end that says, "This is what it means." Art can mean two opposite things. It can mean things that you can't even bring together in your head.

I think art that makes you feel uncomfortable at first is the art you should pay attention to. If it's making you uncomfortable, it's working on you somehow. I think you should ask yourself what's happening and why it makes you feel that way.

Judith Sims: Look at a heck of a lot of art. Really. Put in the time. To develop one's own taste in art, it's essential to make looking a priority. We spend hours shopping to discover what we like, and art requires no less focused attention.

Chris Cowden: Always consider the times. Art responds to the times because it's always of its time. One of the things that people find most distressing about Contemporary Art is that it's aggressive, it's bombastic, it's large, it's noisy. And then you think, "What's our world like right now?" And a lot of today's art is responding to that.

Rohitash Rao: If you really want to see a painting, you have to go to the museum or the gallery. You can't see it online. Online, you can't feel it, you can't see the texture, you can't see the sloppiness of the brushstroke, the blood where they cut themself when they were making that one piece of the sky.

Go to museums alone. It's like going to a movie. You can't have a conversation while the movie's going on. Why would you do that in a gallery?

Anthony Schmitt: Give yourself permission to go on the journey that the artist wants to take you on. Every time you go look at art, there can be an opportunity to experience a new journey because you're giving up what you saw the last time and giving yourself permission to be taken to a completely different place.

Corrina Sephora: Come to it with an open mind. Be curious and prepare to be surprised. Let your curiosity outweigh your judgment.

Lawrence Oliverson: Open your mind and free yourself to attempt to understand what you're looking at. Accept the fact that you may not understand what you're looking at, you may not like it, or you may not agree with it, but that's okay. Just rely on your "gut feelings" and give yourself some extra time to try and understand it.

Rachel Koper: Just respond to the artwork. There's no right or wrong answer. When you ask a hundred people standing in front of an artwork, "What does this remind you of?" you will get ninety-five different answers and five the same. You'd think there would be more overlap, but there isn't.

Barry Whistler: Just get out and see as much as you can. You may not know for yourself what's available until you do that and allow yourself to be exposed to as much different art as you can.

Jamele Wright, Sr.: Have patience. The thing about contemporary work is that every time you see it, you're going to see something different. It's not unlike when you meet someone and each time you talk to them, you find out something new about them.

Rick Allred: The best thing I can advise is to take your time and be curious. You might just discover something that you hadn't planned on.

2) What is it about a Modern Art piece that makes it work (makes it successful)?

These responses give you a glimpse into what art-savvy folks attend to and think about when they're evaluating Modern Art.

Barry Whistler: It's when it moves you in some way, creates some emotion. Sometimes, it takes you to a different kind of place—makes you stop and see things differently. It's as if it has a doorway that presents you with a question, so you're not able to figure it out immediately. It keeps giving.

Bob Adams: What I really look for is authenticity. I try to sense if it feels alive. I think, "How does this work feel to me?"

I also think that it should have a shelf life—it should speak to you differently each time you look at it.

Joshua Kight: Art should have structure, should have unity, but it also should have variety. If there's a lot of unity but no little trip-wires or things you have to think about, you get bored and walk away.

The other extreme of that is when there's no real unity and it's like a cry from the dark of chaos. You get bored with that because you don't see any way in.

When an artist successfully threads that needle between unity and variety, I feel like I'm dealing with an intelligence—a person who's really searching out something. There's a continuing wonderment and puzzle.

Jonathan Tung: I think it's a work that you can look at from many angles, time and time again. It remains relevant as you change. The work becomes a reflection of your experience.

Is it culturally relevant, especially in terms of Contemporary Art? Contemporary Art should be relevant, should be contemporary.

Lawrence Oliverson: I would say that Modern and Contemporary Art is successful when it transcends the original subject matter to stimulate an emotional or intellectual response in the viewer.

Rohitash Rao: I think great pieces of work have a sound. You can hear the clouds moving, hear the energy going through it.

Something about it affects you, and it's not on the logical level.

Sally Weber: Really successful art takes me someplace I've never been before. I can get engaged with the aspects I know and like—color, light, all that stuff—but it's when I'm taken someplace I've never been before, that's the thing.

Aloma Marquis: I ask myself if it is, in some way, satisfying to my eye. Is it satisfying my own personal sense of adventure and my own hungering to know? Do I have an experience of being included in it in some way?

I look to see if it is speaking to anything that's going on in contemporary society now.

Rick Allred: It's all very subjective, but it's when I feel that the person has mastery over their materials. The best way I can describe that is that it looks like they have a developed style.

Becky Hendrick: It engages my eye and then grabs me. It makes me want to figure out what about it is grabbing me.

3) What should I do if I don't like a work of Modern Art?

You might think that art professionals love (or at least like) all the Modern Art they see in highly respected museums and galleries. They don't—but they don't let that stop them from appreciating it and recognizing the impact it has on them. Perhaps their advice will open up some new possibilities for you.

Becky Hendrick: What if it's because you don't know how to like it yet? If a work of art is new to me and I don't know what I'm seeing or hearing, then there's a chance I won't like it because I don't know how to like it yet.

Rick Allred: I would encourage you to read the artist's statement or the project statement.

I think It's important to know why the art was created because then, even though you might not like it, you can appreciate what they're expressing and why they're expressing it. Then you have a connection to it.

Aloma Marquis: Admit that you don't like it. Then, start asking yourself questions. "What is it about this that is disagreeable to me? Is it the formal qualities—are they not acceptable to me? Don't walk away from it until you've interrogated yourself.

Joshua Kight: I think there's art that you can appreciate intellectually but don't really feel on the deepest level. Some work may not resonate with you because you are not carrying around the right raw material inside.

There's some art done by women that's very good. I can understand it intellectually, but because it doesn't relate to my personal experiences, there's a level to it that I'm not getting.

I think that's true of a lot of works of art. You look at them and there's a level to them you're not getting because you're not there. You didn't grow up in West Africa, or you didn't grow up in a repressive Jewish household and rebel against it.

Lawrence Oliverson: You can have a very negative emotional response to something and not like it for that reason but still appreciate it for its success at eliciting that response in you. I think you can very much appreciate the creativity expressed in the new way or the unusual way or the unfamiliar way.

Judith Sims: You don't have to like what the curators at the Guggenheim or the Met like. But you can certainly be interested in their ideas.

Jonathan Tung: Don't totally dismiss any work. As you grow, your experiences grow, and you may not see the work in the same way. I think it's important to revisit and never completely dismiss anything. We all do it, but we shouldn't.

Jamele Wright, Sr.: If you don't like a work, say, "I'm not really sure if I understand it yet," which gives you the opportunity to be wrong. Being wrong sometimes is the gift, because we learn from being wrong. Tomorrow you may find out that what you thought you understood, you didn't.

So to say that you don't like something—give it a few years. Maybe you're not there yet, and that's okay. In fact, that's good because it means that we're ever-evolving, ever-changing, ever-growing. That's what we're supposed to be as people.

To be dismissive of art is to stunt your own growth.

Chris Cowden: It's important to keep in mind that things impact you in different ways. It's not just the piece; it depends on how you're feeling, what you're thinking, how much you're engaged,

Vincent Falsetta: The beauty of being alive on this planet is that we have different people, different races, different genders, different economic issues, different families, different hair, different skin color, different relationships with anger, forgiveness.

I find the beauty in the world of multiple voices.

4) What impact does Modern Art have on you?

In the first chapter, I went to great lengths to let you know why it's worth your while to become a fan of Modern Art. In this chapter, I'm excited to let you in on how art professionals describe the impact that Modern Art has on them. It's my intention that, by reading what they share, you will be more aware of the impact that viewing Modern Art has on you.

Becky Hendrick: It just stops me in my tracks—I have no words for it. It grabs me. Sometimes I get chill bumps. Sometimes I cry. Sometimes I grin. It takes me out of myself.

Aloma Marquis: Joy! Joy and a sense of play. It gives me this powerful access to the unspoken part of life. Language is too limited. Art gives me an unlimited access to that part of myself and life in general.

Vincent Falsetta: I pay attention to how I physically feel. When I walk into a space and it's chilly, and then the sun warms my body, that's a physical response. Sometimes something like that may happen looking at art. It has made me feel like I was standing with better posture. The hairs on my arms would feel like they were doing something. Both my mind and my body respond.

Joshua Kight: Art gives me this cool well-spring of joy that I can revisit at any time. It's this thing that runs underneath whatever temporal events are going on in my life. I have an abiding joy that I carry around from the looking at, experiencing and making of art.

Chris Cowden: It can be uplifting, it can be transporting, it can be transformative. The impact can be about as wide a range as any experience.

Things impact me in different ways. It's not just the piece; it depends on how I'm feeling, what I'm thinking, how much I'm engaged.

Lawrence Oliverson: Art gives me a very uplifting feeling. Sometimes my excitement level rises. I can actually feel my body racing a little bit more when I see something really interesting. I don't mean that it's a strong feeling. It's just a subtle thing.

I hope that the wise and insightful perspectives expressed above have fulfilled their potential to be eye-opening and liberating for you.

As I mentioned earlier, there is an enormous amount of phenomenal art that you won't find in museums or galleries. The works so generously shared by the artists I interviewed are perfect examples of outstanding Modern Art, most of which you won't see elsewhere. Enjoy!

Anthony Schmitt
Shopping Cart Tree
Annual since 1993
Shopping carts, hose clamps,
zip ties and decorations
12 x 33 feet
Courtesy of the Artist

Anthony Schmitt
Band-Aid Trump
May 2020
Mixed media: paper, copy and Band-Aid
11×17 inches
Courtesy of the Artist

Rick Allred
Let It Be Heard
2020
Paper cranes, mixed media
8 x 10 x 8 feet
Courtesy of the Artist

84

Rick Allred
The Beginning
2004
C-Print
16 x 24 inches
Courtesy of the Artist

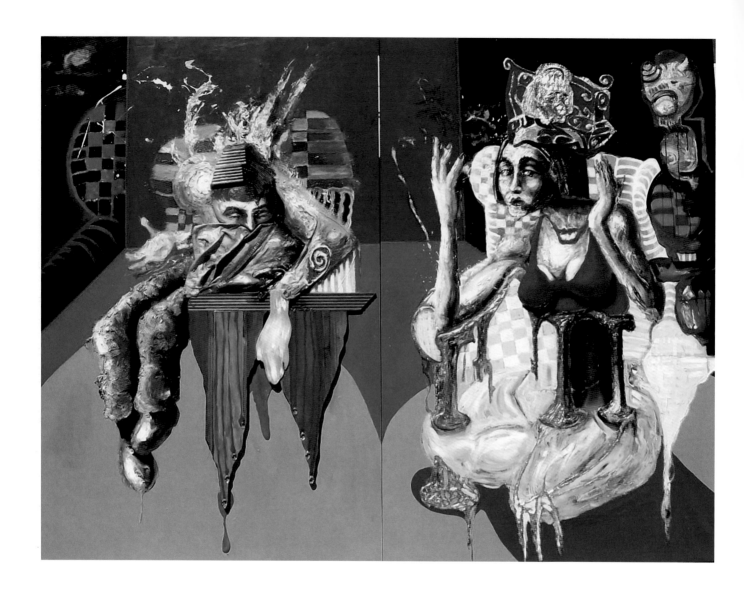

Joshua Kight
Rich Man's Family
2010
Mixed media diptych
6 x 8 feet
Courtesy of the Artist

Joshua Kight
Elephant's Memory
2009
Mixed media
5 x 3 feet
Courtesy of the Artist

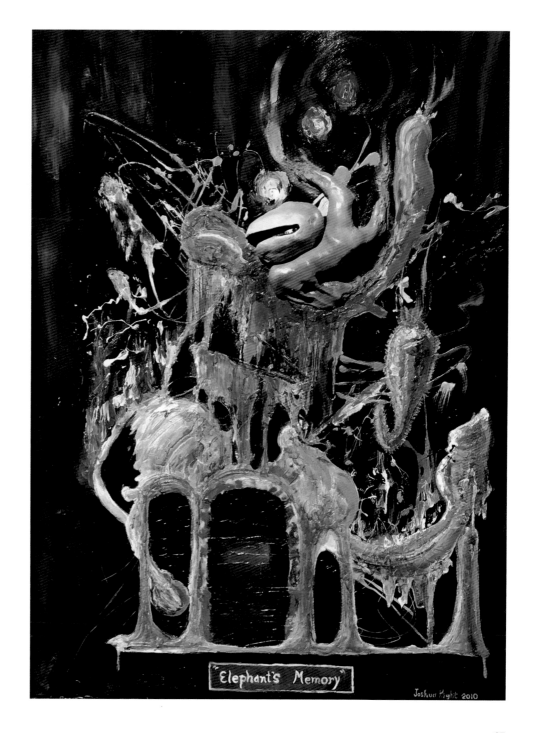

Aloma Marquis
Pray/Prey
2018
Mixed media on paper
17.5 x 22 inches
Courtesy of the Artist

Aloma Marquis
Prophecy
2020
Mixed media collage on paper
25 x 32 inches
Courtesy of the Artist

Rohitash Rao
I Think I'm in Love with You
2017
Acrylic on wood
22 x 70 inches
Courtesy of the Artist

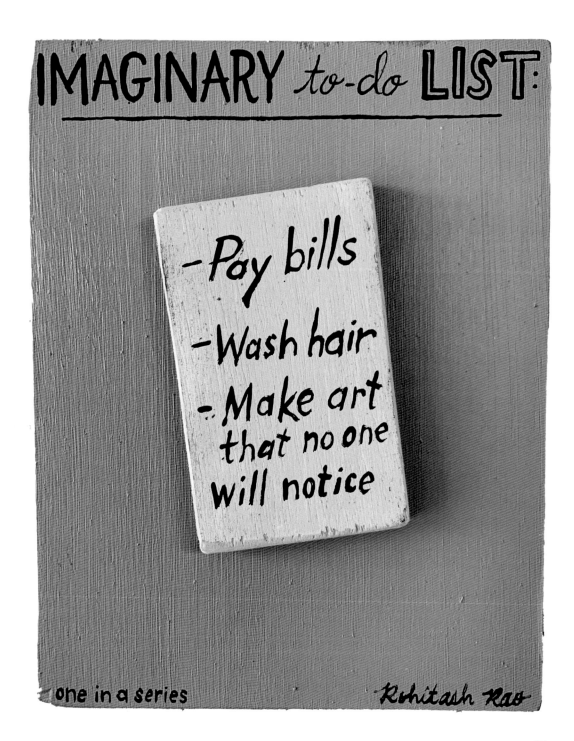

Rohitash Rao
Imaginary To-Do List
(1 in a series)
2020
Acrylic on wood
10 x 12 inches
Courtesy of the Artist

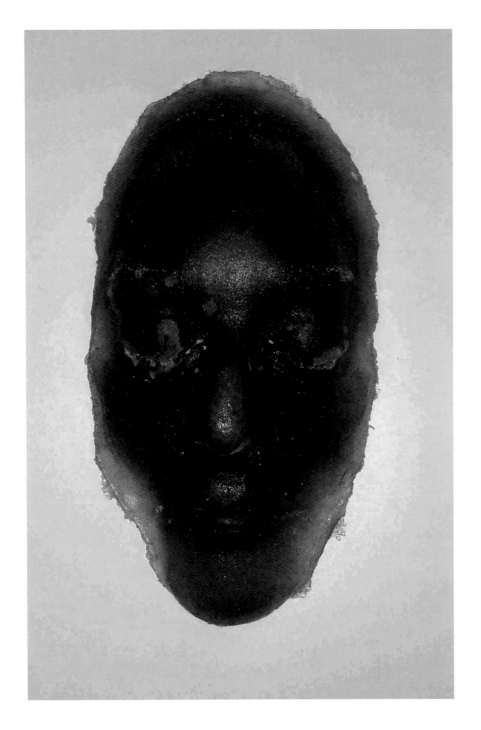

Becky Hendrick
Metamucil Me
2015
Life-cast Metamucil and fiberglas resin
8 inches tall
Courtesy of the Artist

Becky Hendrick
Sweet Leaving
2004
Mixed media
48 x 36 inches
Courtesy of the Artist

Jamele Wright, Sr.
INTRANSIT 18
2020
Mixed media, Georgia red clay,
Dutch wax cloth
48 x 60 inches
Courtesy of the Artist

Jamele Wright, Sr.
ReBORN 1
2020
Mixed Media, Georgia red clay,
Dutch wax cloth
48 x 48 inches
Courtesy of the Artist

Corrina Sephora
Target I
2019
Paper targets, acrylic, pigment on panel
144 x 72 x 2 inches
Courtesy of the Artist

Lawrence W. Oliverson
Untitled
2019
Archival pigment print on paper
22.2 x 28.7 inches
Courtesy of the Artist

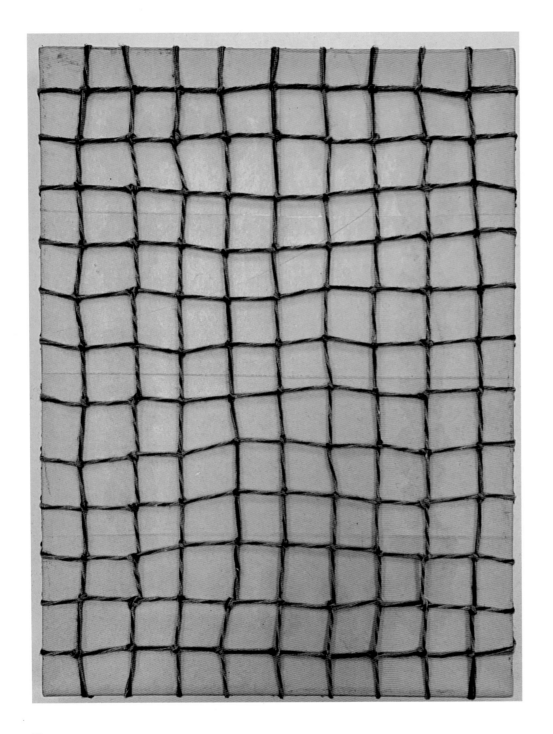

Bob Adams
Untitled
2019
Acrylic, paper,
and cotton cord on canvas
9 x 12 inches
Courtesy of the Artist

Bob Adams
Untitled
2019
Acrylic and yarn on canvas
16 x 20 inches
Courtesy of the Artist

Vincent Falsetta
EZ 20-2
2020
Oil on canvas
63 x 50 inches
Courtesy of the Artist

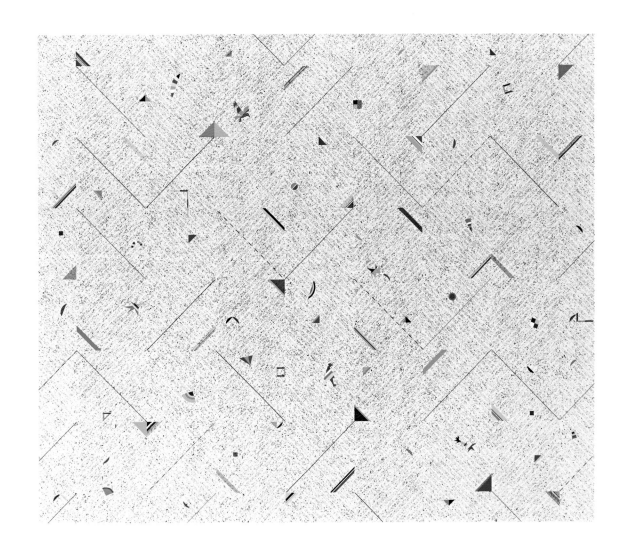

Vincent Falsetta
92-1
1992
Acrylic on canvas
55 x 65 inches
Courtesy of the Artist

Sally Weber
Carbon Rose
2016
Dimensional digital image printed on archival paper
Limited edition
44 x 51 inches
Courtesy of the Artist

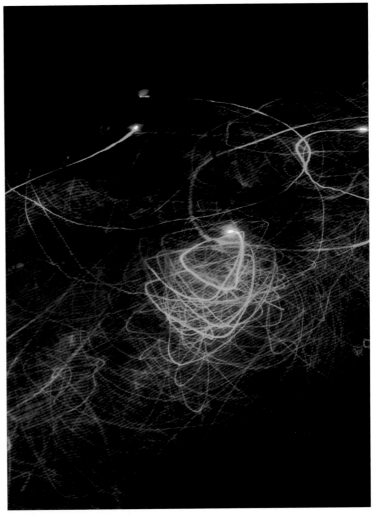

Sally Weber
inFLUX
2021
Site-specific laser pendulum installation
10 x 20 x 10 feet
Courtesy of the Artist

The greatest painting remains always a limitation—an intellectual residue—of a colossal truth much greater than we can recognize.

— Corinne West

PART FOUR

Developing Art Savvy

CHAPTER 14   HOW MODERN ART BEGAN – A TOUCH OF ART HISTORY

I don't know if you have ever wondered (or if you know) how Modern Art began—how art evolved from realistically depicting the world in an aesthetically pleasing way to a virtual free-for-all of expressions. That's what I'm going to talk about in this chapter.

Why didn't art just keep going in the direction it was going? What happened?

True to my intention that this be a non-academic book, I will address what happened in broad strokes. The point is not to give you a lesson in art history but to give you some background that should provide more insight into what set the stage for Modern Art and how Modern Art came to be. (If you're interested in a more detailed account, there are numerous resources available.)

It is generally agreed that the Modern Art era began in the 1860s. There are indisputable facts about what was happening in the Western World at that time, but differing opinions about which factors were the most influential in paving the way for Modern Art to emerge.

For many centuries, art served several basic functions, not the least of which was capturing history. Royal families and aristocrats commissioned artists to memorialize people and historical events; without artists, there would have been no visual record of what the world was like.

The Church has a long history of patronizing artists to illuminate its manuscripts and decorate its shrines with compelling religious images. The Church boasts vast collections of frescoes, paintings, sculptures and stained glass, all for the sake of creating a beautiful, awe-inspiring atmosphere in which to disseminate its message.

Fortunately, the artists of yore were artists—and artists are creative. Even when producing commissioned work with very specific parameters, they brought life and great aesthetic achievement to the task.

Naturally, artists also created art just for the sake of their own enjoyment; in fact, there is an entire category of art called "genre painting" in which artists depicted ordinary people engaged in everyday activities.

What brought about the metamorphosis from realism to the multitude of expressions we call Modern Art? There were many factors, but the one I think is the most pivotal is the invention of the photograph.

Although the camera had been invented centuries earlier, the capability of printing photos was a whole other matter. The first partially successful photograph was produced in 1816 by Joseph Nicéphore Niépce. Although photography developed very quickly from that point, it was only available to professionals and the very rich until George Eastman started a company called Kodak in the 1880s.

So, what difference did the popularization of photography make? Although artists are highly skilled at capturing life realistically, a photograph is obviously much more immediate and has the advantage of undeniable accuracy. As photography became more widespread, artists were no longer required to be the sole recorders of visual history.

I don't know what it was like for artists when photography came onto the scene. Did they feel cheated out of their livelihood? Did they feel liberated? I imagine that the technological breakthrough of photography must have put a lot of artists out of business. In any case, art was on a trajectory that proved to be breathtakingly creative.

No doubt there were some challenges for artists as the world transitioned from traditional to Modern Art. However, if you've known many artists, you have probably noticed that artists find ways to create art regardless of the circumstances. To give you a sense of how that works, I have an example from my own life.

When I was in my twenties, I worked as a recreation instructor for the City of Fort Worth. One of my duties was to teach slip-cast ceramic classes to the blind.

(In case you're not familiar with this craft, and are curious, here's the process. You start with a plaster mold of a shape such as a vase or bowl. You pour clay that has been watered down to a consistency similar to whipping cream, called "slip," into the molds. The water in the liquified clay soaks into the plaster and forms a clay coating on the mold. When this coating has become thick enough, you pour out the excess slip and let the coating dry until it easily comes away from the plaster mold—and voilà! You have a replica of the interior shape of the mold, which you then glaze and fire in a kiln. It's really quite ingenious.)

Typically, the molds are made in shapes like bunny rabbit coffee mugs for Easter and turkey platters for Thanksgiving. This is not to my taste, and I was not happy about teaching that class. However, after a while, I began to find ways to express myself in that medium and, in fact, have a great time doing it. I created whimsical ceramic vases with carved scenes of puffy clouds, bright rainbows and metallic stars amid airbrushed skies. Friends began asking to purchase them.

Over time, I took on the ceramic work as a serious pursuit. I developed my own method of applying transparent layers of color, and created flowing, elegant non-representational paintings on ceramics. Before I knew it, I was making my living creating ceramic pieces, I did this for well over a decade.

Back to the artists of the mid-to-late 1800s. Happily (or unhappily), they found themselves released from the confines of realistic representation, and they ran with it. Well, maybe it would be more accurate to say that they walked with it. Even before the Impressionists hit the scene in the late 1800s, artists had already begun cautiously tiptoeing their way into new modes of expression.

Usually, Impressionism is credited by art historians as being the turning point from traditional to Modern Art. The Impressionists were regarded as renegades. The critics of the time were anything but impressed with the work of these artists. Because their work was rejected by the Salon (the annual French state-sponsored exhibition), they banded together and formed the Anonymous Society of Artists (Société Anonyme des Artistes). This group created their own exhibition and the journalist, Louis Leroy, referred to the artists, insultingly, as "impressionists," and the name stuck.

Looking back, Impressionism may not seem that radical, but at the time, it was a huge departure from convention. Artists were attempting to paint the light. They were not painting the thing itself, but the light!

In 1897, Claude Monet, one of the most renowned Impressionists, began a series of paintings of his garden and its pond with water lilies. Gradually, he became less concerned with traditional pictorial space.

Then, in 1906, Monet produced the painting, *Water Lilies*, in which there was no horizon line at all. This was a very big deal. Why? Because it pioneered new territory. It suggested that artists could paint on the surface of the canvas (the picture plane) without having to make the canvas appear to be a window into three-dimensional reality. The picture could look two-dimensional.

Did Monet's water lily paintings ever look completely flat? No. The water lilies were painted using perspective, so they appear to go back in space. Nonetheless, these works created what I call an "opening" for a new approach to pictorial space.

I can imagine other artists at the time seeing Monet's water lily paintings and wondering, "What would happen if this were taken a step further? What if three-dimensional perspective were abandoned altogether and the picture plane approached in completely new ways?"

It became legitimate for brush strokes to represent only brush strokes. Artists could paint a square rather than a cube, a circle instead of a sphere or even a portrait where the nose is in profile but both eyes are visible!

And so it went. The rest is (forgive me) history!

CHAPTER 15   CRAFTS, FINE CRAFTS, DECORATIVE ART, FINE ART – WHICH IS WHICH AND SO WHAT?

As you know, the purpose of this book is to return you to your natural affinity for Modern Art so that you can have the awe-inspiring experience it offers. In service of that, I want to make sure you know what sets fine art apart from other types of art. After all, Modern Art is fine art.

It can be really perplexing to consider why you should bother to learn to appreciate an Andy Warhol soup can when Aunt Ruth paints perfectly lovely sailboats. Or you may wonder whether a fabulous gown by Christian Dior is considered fine art.

In this chapter, I distinguish the differences among crafts, fine crafts, decorative art and fine art. Being familiar with these classifications will assist you in knowing how to relate to them.

Crafts are functional objects that are made by hand with an intention that they be visually appealing. The term "craft" includes both hobby (or recreational) crafts and fine crafts. Ceramics and glass work, flower crafts, leatherwork, needlework, jewelry, paper crafts, housewares and furniture are among the many varieties of crafts. Crafts are also referred to as "the decorative arts" and "functional art."

Fine Crafts are functional objects designed by artisans (also called artists or craftspeople) and fashioned by hand. Fine crafts are most often made by professionals who have devoted their lives to their craft. For objects to be considered fine crafts, they must show mastery of aesthetics, creativity and structural detail.

Fine crafts can be made of any materials and are often fashioned out of clay, metal, yarn, thread, fabric, wood, leather, stone, glass, plastic, concrete, paper and even masonry. Fine crafts are often made from the finest materials, such as porcelain, gold, silver, bronze, etc.

Fine crafts are often exhibited in art museums, which does not alter the fact that they are fine crafts as distinct from fine art. Why is it significant that they are not fine art? Because the creative possibilities of crafts, no matter how exquisite, are limited by the fact that they must serve a function.

Decorative Art is a category of visual art including, but not limited, to painting, drawing, sculpture and printmaking, whose purpose is—you guessed it—decoration.

Decorative art is often intended to be soothing or festive. It tends to be derivative rather than original, and pleasant and pretty rather than challenging.

Decorative art is sometimes formulaic; by that, I mean that the artists develop their own "recipe" or technique and don't deviate from it. The quality of originality, which is central to fine art, is much less important in decorative art. Decorative art, however, often evidences mastery of technical skill and design.

Frequently, decorative art is done in the style of some by-gone art movement. Impressionism and Cubism are cases in point. A painting executed today in the style of Impressionism or Cubism might be quite lovely, but it doesn't qualify as fine art. Why? The Impressionists were digging deep into their hearts and souls and experimenting with painting the light. They were daring to buck the art establishment of the time. The Cubists were taking risks by experimenting with an innovative way of approaching three-dimensionality. These art movements were phenomenally innovative in their own eras. Doing work in those styles now is, dare I say it, a form of imitation.

For those of us who have been exposed to a great deal of decorative art (and haven't we all—it's what we see in most doctors' offices, hotel lobbies and corporate hallways), it's easy to see how we may have come to believe that all art should look like decorative art. This is especially true if you haven't spent much time in museums and fine galleries and had the opportunity to experience fine art.

It can certainly be argued that decorative art has its place—and in reality, it does. It adorns otherwise plain spaces. But if I had my way, all the art displayed in homes, office buildings, restaurants—well, everywhere—would be fine art and fine crafts rather than decorative art.

Fine Art is an object, group of objects or other display created by an artist primarily for aesthetic and intellectual purposes and designated as art. Fine art has no function except to be experienced by an audience. Originality, creativity and mastery are vital values in fine art. Fine art is thought-provoking as well as emotionally evocative; it invites the viewer to spend time exploring it. It can be a source of delight as well as a challenge to both our senses and our sensibilities.

Like decorative art, fine art can also be decorative. However, fine art always goes beyond mere decoration into the sublime.

Fine art has the singular distinction of being created for no other reason than to satisfy the artist's drive to make art.

Now that I've laid out the "which is which" of four major classifications of art, it's time to answer the question, "So what?" It was important to distinguish between the four kinds of art in this chapter so that you know fine art when you see it. Why does this matter? Because fine art is the only art that will give you the transformative, magnificent experience that I know is possible for you

CHAPTER 16   SOME ART BASICS – A BRUSH WITH TERMINOLOGY

This chapter answers some questions you might have regarding terminology and concepts in art.

ART FORMS

This first category of art terms is related to the various configurations that art takes, I'm certain to have missed some already-existing forms, plus new forms are being invented all the time.

Sculpture: *Three-dimensional art, often intended to be viewed on all sides (usually excluding the bottom or base).*

Sculptures can be constructed from any materials that can be formed into a three-dimensional object.

A subcategory of sculpture is called "relief." In relief sculptures, there are raised elements that remain attached to a solid background of the same material. They are viewed from the front, similarly to a painting.

A "bas-relief" is a type of relief sculpture where the raised portion is very shallow. ("Bas" is a French word meaning "low.")

Drawing: *Two-dimensional artwork produced by making marks, usually on a flat surface, most often paper. The marks are made with mediums such as graphite, ink, charcoal, colored pencils and pastels.*

Drawings are most often black (or graphite-colored) and white. The difference between drawing and painting is generally that painting is done with wet mediums and applied with brushes, palette knives and other tools, while drawing is done with dry mediums.

Of course, there are exceptions, like "pen and ink drawings." Also, there are some people who consider works in pastels (which are dry) to be paintings. The categorization can depend somewhat on how much of the paper shows through. In those artworks considered to be drawings, a considerable amount of the paper or other surface usually shows through.

Painting: *Two-dimensional artwork made by applying paint to a flat surface, such as paper, stretched cloth (often canvas), wood, or metal, etc.*

All paints consist of dry powdered pigments mixed into liquid mediums such as water, oil and water plus acrylic resin. Painting mediums include watercolors, tempera, acrylics, oils, and encaustic (wax).

Printmaking (also called Graphic Art): *Artwork made by using a printing process, usually by transferring ink onto paper.*

Prints involve the transfer of ink or paint from a matrix or through a screen onto a sheet of paper or other material. The matrices are typically: metal or polymer plates for engraving or etching; stone, aluminum, or polymer for lithography; wood for woodcuts and wood engravings; and linoleum for linoleum block prints, also known as linocuts.

Screens made of stretched silk or synthetic fabrics are used to make silkscreen prints, also known as screen printing and serigraphy.

Monoprints can be made by applying paint or ink freehand onto a surface and printing it onto paper.
With the exception of monoprints, printmaking always involves making multiples of the same image.

Collage: *Artwork constructed of various materials, glued onto a flat surface.*

Collages may include such materials as magazine and newspaper clippings, ribbons, paint, ink, colored or metallic papers, other artwork, photos or found objects.

Assemblage: *Artwork made by assembling disparate elements like everyday objects that may have been scavenged or purchased by the artist.*

Assemblages can include things like feathers, scrap wood, leather, shells, cans, stones, etc.

Filmmaking and Video: *An electronic medium for the recording, playback, copying, broadcasting and display of visual moving imagery, usually including sound.*

Although the lines between filmmaking and videography are blurred, filmmaking is generally the term used to describe the whole process of creating a film, including set design, casting and so on, while videography usually refers to the process of using the camera to record the images. Nonetheless, in museums, "moving pictures" are called videos.

Digital Art: *Art made using software, computers, or other electronic devices. Digital art was once known as computer art or new media art.*

Anything produced using digital media, such as animations, photographs, illustrations, videos, and digital paintings, can be classified as digital art.

Installation: *Artwork that consists of more than one "object," where the "objects" can include film/video, sound, light and any other mediums.*

The arrangement of these "objects" in the space is an integral part of the installation. Installations tend to be quite large—often the size of a room or even an entire gallery.

Photography: *Artwork made through the use of a camera and any variation of photographic printing and projection processes.*

Traditionally, photography is printed on paper, but photographic methods and presentation take greater and greater advantage of technological advances to all manner of projection and digital creativity.

Textile Art: *Artwork made through the use of weaving, tapestry, embroidery or other textile processes.*

Although textile work is most often functional and, therefore, considered craft, textiles can also be used as a medium for fine art. Because textile work has been historically the domain of women and kept largely in the field of craft, much feminist art uses textiles for its symbolic meaning.

Mixed Media: *Any artwork made with a combination of mediums.*

In a museum or gallery, the label may specify the various mediums included in the piece or it may simply read, "Mixed Media." Either way is considered acceptable.

Performance Art: *Artwork that is created through actions carried out by the artist and/or other participants, commonly in real time and presented to the public in a fine art context.*

Performance art can contain spontaneous elements or be completely planned. Performance art affords artists the opportunity to include physical movement and to work in an impermanent way.

BASIC ART STYLES

In art, the word "style" applies to everything from an artist's way of making brushstrokes to much broader categories encompassing entire approaches to art. The styles described below are the broad categories.

Realism: *Artwork that is intended to reproduce, either two- or three-dimensionally, what the eye sees.*

Realistic work can be done in any medium, yet is most often seen in drawings, paintings and sculptures.

Photorealism: *Two-dimensional artwork based on photographic images and intended to closely resemble those images.*

Because human beings see through the lenses of two eyes and cameras have only one lens, images produced photographically have a more flattened-out appearance. Close observation of a photo-realistic work of art compared with a realistic work copied from the natural world reveals this difference.

Gallerist and author Louis K. Meisel coined the term "Photorealism" in 1969.

Representational: *Artwork that is intended to depict something recognizable from the real world.*

Representational art includes not only realism but some abstract art, as well. As long as the image is clearly intended to resemble something in the world, it is accurate to call it representational.

Non-Representational or Non-Objective: *Artwork that is not intended to reference anything in the real world at all.*

Non-objective artworks are not meant to depict anything other than themselves. The paint strokes don't represent anything other than paint strokes. The shapes are just shapes, not intended to resemble something from the real world.

The term "non-objective" came into being in 1918 when Alexander Rodchenko titled some of his works simply Non-Objective Painting.

This genre is also referred to as "abstract."

Abstract: *Art that is either not intended to represent external reality at all or intended to represent external reality only loosely.*

So, "abstract" is sometimes synonymous with "non-objective" and "non-representational." At other times, the term "abstract" applies to art in which the images are recognizable as reflecting something in the world, but the images are intentionally altered.

Abstract art is generally agreed to have begun around the early 1900s.

Conceptual Art: *Artwork in which the concept behind the piece is more important than the traditional concerns for form and aesthetics.*

The fact that the concept is the focus of conceptual art does not mean that form and aesthetics are disregarded, but that they are not the main focus. Conceptual art is first conceived, then executed, as distinct from much of other Modern Art, which is conceived in the process of its execution.

Conceptual art is often done in the form of installations (see "Installation" above).

Conceptual art arose in the 1960s.

ART GENRES

Art genres refer to the traditional subject matter of fine art. The term "art genre" applies to all art mediums but is usually used in reference to paintings, drawings and sculptures.

Figurative: *Artwork (regardless of medium or style) that incorporates the human figure.*

This includes both realistic and abstract representations of the figure—clothed or unclothed, two-dimensional or three-dimensional.

Landscape: *Artwork that portrays some form of inland scenery, natural or manmade.*

Landscapes range from being easily recognizable to being very abstract or subtly suggested. They are most often done on a picture plane whose width is greater than its height (hence the paper orientation, "landscape").

Seascape: *Artwork that features a view of the sea or that represents a scene at sea.*

Seascapes can range from being highly abstract to extremely realistic. They are most often done on a picture plane whose width is greater than its height.

Portrait: *Artwork that depicts a specific person through painting, drawing or print-making, showing only the face or the head and shoulders of the subject.*

Portraits can be realistic or abstract, but most are realistic.

Bust: *A three-dimensional (sculptured) representation of a person, which includes only the head and neck and usually part of the shoulders and chest.*

In Western culture, significant figures in history are often memorialized with busts cast in bronze or carved in stone.

Still-Life: *Artwork that represents arrangements of inanimate objects such as books, vases, flowers and fruit, usually on a table in a room.*

Still-lifes are seen as being a very classical and dignified art genre. This has given modern and contemporary artists a wonderful starting point from which to bring playfulness and outside-the-box interpretations.

THE SEVEN VISUAL ART ELEMENTS

In the context of art, the word "formal" refers to all of the visual aspects of a work of art. The formal elements are the components that work together to create an entire visual impression.

If you're looking at a work of art and want to analyze its formal components, distinguishing the individual elements is a good way to do it.

Color: *Color as an element includes both the hue and the saturation, as described below.*

Hue: *This is the color—like blue, orange, etc.*

Hue is determined by the specific wavelength of the light bouncing off of a surface.

Saturation: *This refers to how bright or dull a color is. In a work of art, there is likely to be a range from bright to dull.*

Saturation is also referred to as "intensity" and "chroma."Gray and black are said to be completely unsaturated.

Black is a color which results from the absence or complete absorption of visible light. White is a color which results from the reflection of all the visible wavelengths of light.

Value: *This is how light or dark the color is. White is the lightest value and black is the darkest.*

Almost every work of art has some range of values. Any hue can be made darker or lighter by the addition of white or black. The difference between light and dark values is called "contrast."

Neutrals (black, white and gray) are also said to have value, light to dark.

A tint is a hue to which white has been added. A shade is a hue to which black has been added. A tone is a hue to which gray has been added, specifically a pure gray, made with equal amounts of white and black.

Value is a significant factor in determining the feeling or atmosphere of a work of art.

Texture: *Refers to the surface of the work of art, including both the actual physical surface and the appearance of the surface.*

Texture can be created in any number of ways. For example, texture can be the result of paint application, the inclusion of other objects or materials on the surface, or the inscribing or cutting into the surface of a work of art.

A texture can be smooth, rough, shiny, matte, impasto (very thick with undulations) and so on.

Line: *Lines are marks made by moving a mark-making tool (like a pencil, pen or paintbrush) between two points.*

The viewer can identify the movement that made the line based on the line's direction and how it was applied (fast or slow, for example). Lines can vary in thickness and a single line can have varying thickness.

Lines can describe outlines and exist as design elements as well as create texture.

Shape: *Shapes are formed by lines that are closed and by differentiation of color or value.*

Shapes are generally organized into two categories: geometric and free-form (also called "organic.") They can be hard or soft-edged, as well.

Form: *Form can be said to happen when shape acquires depth.*

Three-dimensional art usually takes the physical form it is intended to be or represent. In contrast, two-dimensional art can convey the illusion of form through the use of perspective or shading or both.

Space: *Space refers to the areas within, between and around the shapes within a piece.*

Space can appear to be two-dimensional or three-dimensional. Three-dimensional space can seem to be flat, shallow or deep.

The space within a shape or depicted object is called "positive," whereas the space around shapes or objects is called "negative."

The use of positive and negative space in the composition of a work of art is important to how interesting the piece is.

OTHER USEFUL TERMS

These are a few of the most frequently-used terms in reference to art.

Scale: *This is the size of the work of art.*

The scale of a work of art affects its impact, as does the scale relative to its subject matter and the size of the shapes within the piece compared to the overall size of the piece.

Composition: *The way the visual elements are arranged in relation to one another and sometimes to the space in which the work is displayed.*

Compositions are often based on "design principles." These are formulas that are considered to be foolproof methods to achieve successful compositions. They include "symmetry," the "rule of thirds" and the "golden mean." However, contemporary artists often break these rules for the sake of creating new, fresh compositions.

One time-honored technique for gauging the effectiveness of a composition is to notice what your eye is drawn to and how it moves as you look at the piece. Ideally, your eye will move throughout the work and stay within it without getting stuck in any one place. The longer you find yourself engaged with a piece, the more successful the composition is considered to be.

Medium: *A material that is used to create a work of art.*

Despite the fact that there are traditional mediums such as pencil on paper, oil on canvas and carved stone, artists use a vast array of mediums to create art, especially Modern Art.

In reference to art, the plural of "medium" is most often "mediums" as opposed to "media," which refers to mass communication.

Art Movement: *A direction or mode of artistic exploration that characterizes the art of a specific era and/or place.*

Art movements are given descriptive titles that embody their approaches, ideals and stylistic tendencies. One art movement you've read about in this book is Impressionism. You might also be familiar with Pop Art and Surrealism, both of which are examples of art movements.

As is the case with any discipline, profession or area of study, art is rich with both intellectual concepts and practical information.

The information in this chapter is the tip of the iceberg when it comes to the body of knowledge on the topic of art. In addition to the internet as a source of further information, I also recommend some excellent books in the bibliography.

A word of caution: There is no absolute authority on art terminology, so you will find variations and discrepancies galore among the myriad sources. To complicate matters even further, the definitions of art terms vary somewhat from country to country.

If you're curious, I encourage you to indulge your curiosity. It can be fascinating fun to learn about art!

CHAPTER 17   MEANING – IS THERE ANY?

I debunked the Counterproductive Belief, "Every work of art has a specific, fixed meaning," in Chapter 5. I stand by that debunking. However, I would be remiss if I didn't let you know that there are certain caveats on the subject of meaning.

This book is about learning to love Modern Art, especially the Modern Art that began around the 1940s. To keep it simple, I have referred to all of it as Modern Art, which works just fine until we get into the question of meaning. To do justice to the subject of meaning, I need to separate Modern Art into two types of art— Modern and Contemporary.

Technically, the art that had its roots in Impressionism—which took hold around the 1940s and gradually petered out in the 1960s and 70s—is now labeled Modern Art or Modernism. During that period, accurate representation and meaning were discouraged. Art was meant to be about its visual elements—color, shape, form, space, texture, line, value—and beauty. So, when you're looking at non-representational or abstract art from that period, it's useful to know that it was intentionally devoid of accurately depicted subject matter and meaning.

It was not, however, devoid of feeling. On the contrary. If you look at the work produced during that time frame, it's impossible not to be aware that the art of that period was emotionally evocative.

Modern Art came to an end in the 1960s and 70s and the new period became known as Contemporary Art. Contemporary Art explores the complexities of everyday life through its incredibly diverse and often technologically-advanced mediums. (There are many sub-categories within Contemporary Art, such as Postmodernism, but to keep it simple, I'm referring to all of them as Contemporary Art.)

When it comes to meaning, the distinction between Modern and Contemporary Art is significant. Unlike Modern Art, Contemporary Art is often realistic and is based on some concept. Some of it could even be said to contain a meaning, although not a meaning that you can nail down in words. The meaning is more akin to an open-ended exploration than a concrete pronouncement. Comparing it to literature, meaning in contemporary art is more like poetry than prose.

My own artwork, which, of course, is Contemporary Art, deals with questions of humanity through the lens of women's equality issues. The visual elements of the work are aesthetically pleasing, while the content invites the viewer to think about women—their bodies, their concerns and their place in society. Since the meaning is not spelled out, it remains ambiguous, allowing each viewer's experience to be personal to them.

I think it is wonderful that Contemporary Art is intellectually engaging as well as viscerally and emotionally evocative. But don't get hung up on trying to figure out the exact meaning or trying to interpret it "correctly." That can seriously interfere with the pure joy of being with the art.

A case in point: I have been a fan of Piet Mondrian's work for decades and only recently came upon the theory that his rectangles and lines were meant to represent his vision for an orderly, utopian society. Knowing this is interesting, but I certainly never felt like I was lacking anything in my appreciation for his work before.

I recommend that, in any case, you enjoy the work at face value. There's always something to be gained by being with art. Let both the visual aspects and the subject matter "work their magic on you," so to speak—which could result in insights and openings for hours, days, months or even years to come.

Appreciating art is a personal experience—one where you, the viewer, have your own connection with the art. Ultimately, it doesn't matter what meaning the artist (or anyone else) thinks you should glean from the art. The value for you is in your experience of the art. Period.

CHAPTER 18   A FEW WORDS ON ART CRITICISM AND THE ART MARKET – SHOULD YOU CARE?

I must confess that I was ambivalent about including these topics, given that this book is about how to love Modern Art. I don't know that this information will add to your ability to love Modern Art, but maybe it will answer a question or two in the back of your mind.

I assume that, if you're reading this book, you came to it as someone who felt at least somewhat alienated from the world of Modern Art. If I'm correct, I doubt that you're overly concerned with art criticism—or, for that matter, with the art market.

And yet, there's this little nagging voice in my head telling me not to avoid these topics because you might want to know a little bit about them.

So, here's a little bit on each.

Art Criticism

Most art criticism is heady stuff. Like crossword puzzles, it takes practice to get the hang of it. Art criticism is fascinating to some people. When it's done well, it can provide an intellectually stimulating analysis and even help you see aspects of the art in question that you hadn't considered.

But, is it necessary to read an art critic's assessment in order to get the low-down? Certainly not. That's just one person's opinion. Will it enhance your experience of the art? I don't know. It depends on the critic, I suppose, and your personal predilections—not to mention your mood and numerous other subjective factors.

If you're drawn to reading art criticism, go for it. One word of caution though. I don't recommend you read a review of an exhibit before seeing the work yourself; it's almost impossible not to be influenced by what you read. It could either dissuade you from seeing the art show or put a damper on your appreciation of an exhibit you might otherwise have enjoyed immensely. Even if the review is favorable, it could set you up to be disappointed if your taste differs from the critic's or lead you to discount your own impression of the work.

As I've expressed many times in this book, the joy of Modern Art is in your personal experience of it.

The Art Market

When it comes to the art market, I think the easiest way to get a fix on how it functions is to compare it to other parts of our culture where only a few rise to fame. Think Hollywood and the music industry. It's all a matter of fashion, and fashions come and go. Stardom is very often fleeting, and stardom in the art world is no exception.

Outrageously expensive art has become a huge status symbol among the ultra-rich. There are actually people who compete with one another to pay more than anyone else for a work of art or to own the most costly art collection. There's a very revealing documentary on the topic entitled, *The Price of Everything.*

There are also much less rarified levels of the art market, but fashion still rules. This explains why you can go to prominent galleries in different cities and see similar art and even art done by the same artists.

In short, the art market is a fickle thing. If you're buying art as an investment, it's important to be aware that an artist may be a hot commodity in one moment and forgotten the next.

I was married to an art dealer for several years and spent quite a bit of time with other art dealers. They all gave the same sane advice to people who wanted to purchase art: buy art that you love and don't worry about the past or future value of it. That's the best way to be happy with the art you buy.

Art criticism and the art market are at the bottom of my list of things you would ever need to know about in order to love Modern Art. However, because they are part of the whole realm of Modern Art, touching on them seemed like a good thing to do.

CHAPTER 19 MAKE THE MOST OF MUSEUMS AND GALLERIES – SOAR WITH YOUR MODERN ART WINGS

Now that you've done the work to get to this point, I hereby grant you your "Modern Art Wings." It's time to fly—fly to galleries, fly to museums, maybe even fly to far-away places to see art! Why not become a Modern Art frequent flyer?

If you want to really spread your wings, I challenge you to attend the most progressive, unfamiliar, "edgy" art exhibits you can find.

Don't forget that you have The Magic of Modern Art Tour at your disposal, which gives you a great way to conduct your own self-guided Modern Art tour. I hope and trust it will serve you well in your Modern Art adventures from now on. Instructions for the tour are available In Chapter 11, in Appendix A, and also online at www.MagicOfMagicArt.com/OnTheGo.

Or, when you're in the mood for a different approach, you can take one or more of the suggestions in Chapter 12, "Alternate Approaches – Other Modern Art Tours to Try" (also available online at www.MagicOfModern. com/OnTheGo and Appendix B).

There are so many ways you can motivate yourself to get out and see Modern Art. One of my favorites is to join a Modern Art museum and enjoy the many benefits of membership. If there's no Modern Art museum in your area, join the general art museum, which will also include a Modern Art collection and traveling exhibits.

Museum members receive advance notice of exhibits, openings, talks and events. They get free or discounted admission to the museum, often including special exhibits admission. Another benefit of membership is the opportunity to become part of a community of Modern Art enthusiasts. All of this will help you expand and deepen your own appreciation for the art.

By the way, as a museum member, you also get discounts in the museum stores. They offer beautiful, high-quality gifts for yourself and others, like art books, decorative household items, jewelry, accessories and creative toys for kids. About eighty percent of my earring collection was purchased at art museum gift shops!

Whether or not you join a museum, all of those activities are still available. And most, if not all museums, have some time during each week when the admission is free, which is the ideal time to take the whole family. More and more museums have the most delightful areas full of interactive, often high-tech art activities for children—and let me tell you, they're pretty darned fun for adults, as well!

Besides all this, museums offer other art-related activities like artist talks, film presentations and panel discussions. These are sometimes offered as a series and sometimes as one-time events. You can get on the museums' mailing lists without joining the museums. If you prefer to learn about local offerings as a whole, local periodicals and websites are packed with such information.

Galleries and local art centers provide great benefits, too. Not only do they offer opportunities to see Modern Art at no charge, but they often feature work by local artists. This means that you get to meet artists from your own community. Having conversations with them, as well as with other visitors, can be quite stimulating and thought-provoking. Plus, you could end up with a whole new circle of friends centered around the world of Modern Art.

I wholeheartedly encourage you to create social occasions that include art. For example, instead of going to dinner and a movie, you could go to dinner and a Modern Art opening. Or, consider a lunch date with a friend at a museum. Museum cafes, which are known for their gracious ambiance and delicious food, are the perfect place to enjoy a delicious lunch while you discuss the artwork you just saw.

As with any pursuit, the more time you spend (or, as I like to say, "indulge") in experiencing Modern Art, the more rewarding it becomes. Besides that, your ability to discern the subtle aspects and impact of Modern Art—visually, intellectually and emotionally—expands through exposure.

As you spend more time and come to feel more relaxed with Modern Art, your sense of connection and awe are likely to deepen. You will find yourself in touch with the highest expression of your own humanity. It's addictive in the best possible way.

Great art is great because it inspired you greatly.
If it didn't, no matter what the critics, the museums
and the galleries say, it's not great art for you.

— Yoko Ono

PART FIVE

Curating Your Own
Art Collection

CHAPTER 20   ACQUIRING MODERN ART – HOW TO CHOOSE ART FOR YOUR HOME

Now that you're falling in love with Modern Art—you are, aren't you?—you might want to own some. Having art in your space creates an enlivened atmosphere and, most importantly, feeds your soul.

If you're going to acquire Modern Art, I think it's smart to have guidelines about how to do it. Or, if you already own some, you could be looking to expand your collection. Either way, I'd like to offer you some unasked-for advice.

I'm not going to go into great detail, nor will I address the best strategy for purchasing exclusive high-end art. I just want to give you some general guidelines and food for thought.

Where Not to Buy

At least as important as knowing where to purchase art is knowing where and from whom not to purchase it.

I'll begin with one of the prime culprits—cruise ships. I strongly recommend that you avoid making art purchases on cruise ships, even (or especially) if you have had a few complimentary drinks and are feeling very relaxed about spending money.

The prints for sale on cruise ships are, by most standards, extremely overpriced and are not on a par with artists' prints that are sold in galleries. In fact, they are mass-produced in print shops the same way posters are.

The biggest player by far in the cruise ship art auction world, with more than $300 million in annual revenue and nearly 300,000 artworks sold each year, is Park West Gallery, based in Southfield, Michigan. It handles such a high volume of art sales at sea that it bills itself as "the world's largest art dealer." Park West sells art on the Royal Caribbean, Celebrity, Norwegian, Carnival, Disney, Holland America, Regent and Oceania lines. (Princess runs its own auctions in-house.)

I found an eye-opening article in a 2016 *Bloomberg Businessweek* about Park West, titled, "Ever Bought Artwork on a Cruise Ship? Prepare to be Seasick." Here is an informative but disturbing excerpt.

> Mostly, Park West doesn't sell works that are unique in the sense that most casual collectors might understand. With a few high-end exceptions, it sells what are essentially reproductions with individual embellishments, such as a signature. The official terms include giclée, a type of inkjet print; serigraph, or silk-screen; and "mixed media," which, in most of the Peter Max works, are paper lithographs with dabs of paint added. It took days of me hanging around the gallery and attending auctions to understand this—and I've covered art sales for years as a journalist, with the benefit of a Ph.D. in archaeology. (Vernon Silver 12-14-2016)

I also don't recommend you buy Modern Art from your friend who decided to become an artist last month, unless you get it at an excellent price, preferably free. This may sound snobbish on my part, but it takes very talented artists many years to develop their skills and their unique "voices" as artists.

Georgia O'Keefe is quoted as saying when she was 40 years old and about to have a retrospective exhibit of her work, "The notion that you can make an artist overnight, that there is nothing but genius, and a dash of temperament in artistic success is a fallacy. Great artists don't just happen, any more than writers, or singers, or other creators."

Furthermore, any time you feel pressure to buy, run the other way. The same holds true in any situation where you're being plied with alcoholic drinks at the same time as being encouraged to purchase art on the spot.

Where *to* Buy and Why

My recommendation is that the overriding motivation for you to purchase Modern Art (or any art) is because you adore it. Although people buy art for a variety of reasons—as an investment, to impress others, to support artists through patronage, as decoration to match the sofa, and for the simple love of the art—I stand by my recommendation. As long as you love it, there's no reason why it shouldn't also be an excellent investment, while at the same time, supporting talented artists and impressing your friends.

As for where and from whom to buy it, it's great to purchase Modern Art from reputable galleries anywhere, and especially those in your own community, for obvious reasons.

I encourage you to purchase artwork from your friends who are experienced professional artists and who have grown and developed as artists over some time.

If you're in the economic stratum that would allow you to purchase art from the major art auction houses, go for it.

How Much to Pay

Another aspect of acquiring art is knowing how much to pay for it. Oh, boy. Art prices are unavoidably subjective, and they vary astronomically.

In the upper echelons of the art market, fashion is the determiner of price. The same artist's work can go for vastly different prices at different points in their career, depending on how popular their work is at any given time.

A word of caution about purchasing art for investment purposes; the art market is fickle and unpredictable. There's never a guarantee that a particular artist's work will appreciate in value or even maintain its current value. Most artists, even if they achieve fame and fortune, don't remain famous throughout their lifetimes. However, as you might already know, art tends to appreciate after an artist has died. Vincent Van Gogh is the "poster child" for this phenomenon.

But most of us aren't in that upper echelon and are unlikely to be overly concerned about the investment aspect of purchasing Modern Art. I reiterate my earlier assertion: the key is choosing art you love.

Even so, when purchasing art you love, I'm sure you want to be wise about the money you are spending. I think a good thing to do in advance of considering a specific purchase is to set a firm budget. This will help you avoid a couple of pitfalls.

One pitfall is choosing the least expensive art you can find. Having a budget means you are giving yourself permission to purchase a work at the top end of your budget. This should assist you in making your choice based on your taste, not your pocketbook.

The other pitfall (and this may be surprising) is to go for a particular work of art because it carries a high price tag. You might think that just because a work is expensive means that it's superior and that it's going to hold its value or appreciate in value.

Once you have set the budget, you're ready to shop for just the right artwork for you. You can do so freely because you already know how much you're willing to spend. Whether you already have an artist in mind whose work you'd love to own or you are completely open, enjoy yourself! What a great excuse to look at lots of Modern Art!

So let's say you have found some art that you're considering buying. How do you know if it is priced fairly? Ultimately, it's all subjective, but here are some thoughts that might prove useful.

The first thing to know is that many artists themselves have extreme difficulty pricing their work. So it should come as no surprise if you are uncertain about what a fair price is for any given piece. Gallerists and art dealers can be your best allies in terms of pricing; they are knowledgeable about the art market, including artists' work, their history, their contemporaries and so on.

But, bottom line—how do you quantify and monetize aesthetic value? The best advice I can offer is this: Do whatever due diligence seems appropriate; then, pay whatever you're comfortable paying for that work of art you love. And once you own it, don't look back. Just enjoy your art!

Having art around you connects you to the world of creativity, one of the highest expressions of humanity. Not only will it enhance *your* life, but the life of everyone who gets to see it in your home.

CHAPTER 21   DISPLAYING YOUR ART COLLECTION – PRESENT IT LIKE A PRO

I have had lots of instruction and tons of practice installing Modern Art. When I worked at the Modern Art museum in Fort Worth, I loved being given the opportunity to assist the installation crew on large projects. I expanded this expertise during both undergrad and graduate school and gained even more practice while married to an art dealer. I'm eager to share some of the essentials I learned along the way.

As I mentioned before, I'm not a fan of purchasing art to match the decor. I much prefer that art be chosen on its own merit. I remember being delighted when, during my first trip to New York City, I walked into a posh hotel and came upon a room furnished in French Provincial furniture with Modern Art hung on the walls. It looked fantastic! This experience in one of the most sophisticated and art-savvy cities in the world illustrated in no uncertain terms that art speaks for itself. Any style of fine art can be placed effectively with any style of decor.

Furthermore, in my opinion, art selections are way too personal and, dare I say, sacred, to think of them as mere design elements. I don't want my art to blend in with the decor; I want it to stir my soul.

Anyone who has seen a beautifully curated show in a museum or gallery knows the difference that presentation makes. There are some tried-and-true ways to ace the presentation of *your* art collection, as well as some things to avoid.

Framing

Let's talk about framing. Frames have two functions: they protect the art and they showcase it.

Here are a few dos and don'ts—don'ts first. Don't ever ever ever use a colored mat around any work of art. Ever. A colored mat will alter the appearance of the colors in the art piece. The point of a mat is to create a neutral visual space around the art so as to present the art to its full advantage. I strongly suggest using white or, occasionally, off-white mats.

I recommend that the bottom portion of the mat be wider than the sides and top. If it's not wider, the mat will appear to be thinner on the bottom than the other three sides. A mat that is wider at the bottom also adds a feeling of weight so that the work of art looks grounded. (By the way, there is disagreement about whether or not to make the bottom side of the mat wider than the other three sides. Some say it's an old-fashioned and obsolete convention, but I much prefer it.)

This brings me to another point. Use a first-rate framer. Such a framer provides "museum-quality" framing, also known as "conservation-grade," which helps preserve the art as well as show it off. Proper framing prevents discoloration, fading, acid burn and other damage to the artwork.

Museum-quality framers use only acid-free paper and mat board, as well as glass or acrylic with UV protection. They also ensure that the art is sealed so as to prevent dirt and moisture from getting in. Their excellent craftsmanship not only looks impeccable but also keeps the work of art securely in place to avoid slippage.

Beyond that, a great framer gives you personalized attention, assisting with your selection and showing you a preview of how well a particular mat and frame will complement your piece. My framer has a mirror on the ceiling, which is wonderful because I can look up at the mirror to see how the framed piece will look from several feet away.

You may be wondering about other options for getting your art framed. There are galleries that do framing, but I personally favor a framer that does nothing but framing. However, if you purchase a work of art from a gallery that also does framing, it's very convenient to have your art framed where you purchased it.

Hobby art stores also offer framing services, but I don't recommend using them. Although the frames done by hobby art stores may look fine, they don't provide the same level of preservation for your art, and the prices aren't that much lower.

Because materials and methods are continually being improved, check with your framer to make sure that you can disassemble your framed art to exchange the current materials for upgraded ones in the future.

As for the style of frame to use with Modern Art, I prefer simple, clean lines, but I've seen Modern Art displayed in all styles of frames including very ornate ones. I suggest you let your professional framer assist you with your style choices.

I won't kid you; top-quality professional framing is a significant expense. So be sure to figure in the cost of framing when you purchase a work of art. A high quality frame is well worth the investment in the long run.

The Mechanics of Hanging Art

The mechanics of hanging art might seem obvious, but if you don't know what you're doing, you can hit some snags. Here are some tips that can ensure a smooth, successful hanging process.

First of all, make sure the piece is fitted with a hanging wire that goes horizontally across the back of it. Ideally, the wire is attached one-third of the way down from the top of the piece, including the frame and has some slack to allow for easy hanging.

Always—let me say that again—*always* hang artwork from two hooks. The reason to use two hooks is so you can level the piece and not try to balance it on one center hook. (Those "sawtooth hangers" with the row of pointy triangles are not much better than one hook.)

Hang the hooks at the same height and figure out how far apart and how high on the wall to place them. You will determine this based on the width of the piece, the amount of slack you have in the hanging wire and how far below the top of the artwork the wire comes. When you adjust the piece to make sure it's level after you've hung it on the wall, be sure to lift the piece up slightly as you move it so as not to pull the hooks out of the wall accidentally.

And finally, use good picture-hanging hooks. Do not use nails. Don't even think about using tacks or push pins. I recommend the picture-hanging hooks with the really thin nails because you can move them around without ruining your sheetrock.

Don't worry if you don't get it exactly right the first time—it takes some practice to get a feel for this process.

Placement

If I could change one thing about the way art is displayed in many homes and offices, I would hang it lower. All too often, the art is hung so high that you can't see it clearly, and it appears distorted. Besides, who wants to crane their neck to see the art? It should seem obvious that, in order to receive the full impact of art, you need to be able to see it clearly.

The rule of thumb regarding the optimal height to hang art is to place it so that one-third of the piece is above eye level and two-thirds are below. This formula works most of the time, but what about the fact that people are all different heights? Not a problem. Use an approximate average of the adults in your household (except, of course, in your kids' rooms, where you hang it according to their height).

There are some caveats to this guideline about optimal hanging height. One is that you should take the ceiling height into account. For rooms with extra-high ceilings, hang the art somewhat higher and for low ceilings, somewhat lower. There is not an exact formula for this, so if you have extra-high or extra-low ceilings, experiment with the height of the piece until it looks and feels right and you can still see the art easily.

Avoid the temptation to hang large, vertically-oriented works of art above a sofa. That would make the top of the work too high to see (plus, it just looks wrong). It's better to hang smaller pieces or landscape-oriented works over your sofa and find a different spot for that five-foot-tall portrait.

Another caveat to the rule about height applies if you're hanging a large number of pieces "salon style." Salon style is a method of arranging a group of artworks in which the pieces are hung next to and above each other on a single wall. So, if you are hanging a group of artworks salon style, some of the pieces are probably going to be hung higher than eye level and some below it, and that's perfectly fine.

The last caveat to the height guideline is this: If there's a piece you must have because your heart cries out for it, yet you simply don't have the ideal spot for it, please hang it however you can and ignore all the rules!

Something else to consider when you're hanging art is how far back you need to be in order to see it to its best advantage. For example, I have a four-foot square self-portrait that has a layer of text painted across it.

(A photo of this painting is on the back cover of this book.) You can't discern the face without getting back a few yards, so the painting has to be hung where the viewer can get far enough away for the image of the face to emerge. I also have a small, finely-detailed pencil drawing that calls for being seen up close. Rather than display it where there's lots of room to get back from it, I put it in a spot that's conducive to looking at it up close. This work is hung on the wall in my stairwell.

What about spacing? How much space do you need between one work of art and another? How much space do you need between a single piece (or multiple pieces) and the edge of a wall? Generally, it isn't advisable to hang art all the way to the edge of a wall. It feels claustrophobic. Art spaced too far apart, however, can look disjointed.

As you can tell, art presentation is a complex topic. There are numerous sources of information that delve more deeply into the technicalities of art display. Fortunately, there are professionals you can hire to assist you with the arrangement and actual process of hanging the art in your home. This could be an excellent (though not inexpensive) option. If you don't find anyone in your area when you search for "art hanging service," I suggest you call around to local galleries. They may have someone on their staff who will do it or they might have a recommendation.

Preservation

Although preservation is technically not part of the topic of art presentation, I want to offer some pointers about taking care of your art so it will give you (and, quite possibly your descendants) years and years of enjoyment.

Think of your art as being somewhat fragile. Art may withstand neglect for a while, but if you don't take care of it, it will deteriorate much sooner than necessary.

Here are some guidelines to assist you in caring for your art.

- Keep it clean by dusting it gently and, when needed, by cleaning it with a damp cloth. Microfiber works great.
- Glass and acrylic can be cleaned as you would any glass or acrylic. I also use a damp microfiber cloth for this.
- Avoid direct sunlight, which makes the colors fade, especially reds.
- Manage the temperature. Generally, experts say the temperature should be between 65 and 75 degrees, and some say it should ideally be 70 to 72 degrees.
- Monitor the humidity. The sweet spot is generally agreed to be around 50 percent.
- Perhaps most important, though, is that you keep the temperature and humidity steady.
- Big swings back and forth are bad news for artwork, especially paintings.
- Air quality also affects art. A good air filter goes a long way.
- For wood sculpture, tend to the wood as you would any fine wooden furniture.

Your art is worth caring for. The better you take care of it, the longer it will bring you joy and delight.

Modern Art graces every room of our house, and most of the pieces are my own creations. I enjoy the "oohs" and "aahs" I hear from just about everyone who enters our home.I'm proud of the way my work affects people, and I'm absolutely clear that the way I display it maximizes its impact.

It is often said that curating art is an art form unto itself. The choices of which art to display with which other art, as well as how and where to display it, make a huge difference on the effect the art has on the audience. You are the curator of your art collection. Have fun being creative in the way you curate it!

I think I've made it abundantly clear that my fondest wish is for you to become as wild about Modern Art as I am. As I shared in the introduction, I am committed that this book provide what you need so that your visits to Modern Art exhibits become joyful, enriching experiences—experiences that you eagerly anticipate, avidly soak in and never get over.

I want you to know that wherever you are at this moment in relationship to Modern Art is absolutely perfect. Whether you already loved Modern Art when you started reading this book, or had all but written it off entirely, I invite you to think of your relationship with Modern Art from this moment forward as a new journey, a new exploration.

Have you ever heard the expression, "Trust the process?" It means that, whenever you take on an area of development for yourself, regardless of how it seems along the way, the process is working on you, and it will all turn out. I assert that this applies to you right now, as you rediscover and develop your innate ability to appreciate Modern Art.

You've done the "book learning." All there is to do now is to spend some time with Modern Art. Visit Modern Art exhibits and take yourself on The Magic of Modern Art Tour. Try the alternative approaches. Bring curiosity and wonder to each piece of art you see.

Once again, I invite you to visit *The Magic of Modern Art On The Go* web page. It includes The Magic of Modern Art Tour and two alternate art tours. Just type MagicOfModernArt.com/OnTheGo into your search engine. You can also get there by clicking on the link on your digital device or by using the QR code below. These tours are also included as Appendices A and B at the back of this book.

146

I also encourage you to take advantage of the Magic of Modern Art website, MagicOfModernArt.com. Listen to the theme song. Subscribe to the blog. Share your thoughts and experiences on the discussion board.

You can also visit our Facebook page, Facebook.com/Magic of Modern Art.

Finally, I would love to hear from you about what has opened up in your relationship to Modern Art as a result of reading this book. I invite you to email me at Robyn@MagicOfModernArt.com.

I wish you many ridiculously rewarding hours with Modern Art.

Here's to The Magic of Modern Art!

P.S. Join me! There's more to this than just a book. I'm spearheading a movement whose mission is for everyone everywhere to experience the magic and wonder of Modern and Contemporary Art. This book is an essential tool for the fulfillment of this mission.

If you want to be part of the movement or have questions about it, I would love to talk with you. Please email me at Robyn@MagicOfModernArt.com.

I'm always interested in new venues for delivering Magic of Modern Art talks and doing book signings. If you have a connection or even a suggestion for such a place, please let me know right away!

QR code to MagicOfModernArt.com/OnTheGo

The References are the sources for some of the specific information that is included in this book.

The Resources are materials that I recommend for their potential to inform, forward and enhance your explorations of Modern Art.

As you might imagine, I used many other sources of information just to confirm dates, terminology and so forth. They aren't referred to in the book and are not listed below.

REFERENCES

The Educational Value of Field Trips

Green, Jay P., Bowen, Daniel H., Kisida, Brian, 2016, Education Next, Research, The Journal, Volume 14, No. 1.

The Educational Value of Field Trips

https://www.educationnext.org/he-educational-value-of-field-trips/

How Art Changes Your Brain: Differential Effects of Visual Art Production and Cognitive Art Evaluation on Functional Brain Connectivity

Bolwerk, Anne, Mack-Andrick, Jessica, Lang, Freider R., Dörfler, Arnd, Maihöfner, Christian, July 1, 2014

How Art Changes Your Brain: Differential Effects of Visual Art Production and Cognitive Art Evaluation on Functional BrainConnectivityhttps://journals.plos.org/plosone/article?id=10.1371/journal.pone.0101035

The Benefits of Art on Memory and Creativity

Invaluable, In Good Taste, April 17, 2018

The Benefits of Art on Memory and Creativity

https://www.invaluable.com/blog/benefits-of-art

Inside the Strange World of Cruise Ship Art Auctions

Format Magazine, Genista Jurgens, June 18, 2017

Inside the Strange World of Cruise Ship Art Auctions

https://www.format.com/magazine/features/art/cruise-ship-art-auctions-controversy

RESOURCES

***Getting It*: A Guide to Understanding and Appreciating Art**

Becky Hendrick, 1999, Published by Becky Hendrick

Seeing Slowly: Looking at Modern Art

Michael Findlay, 2017, Prestel Publishing

History of Modern Art: Painting, Sculpture, Architecture, Photography

H.Harvard Arnason, Elizabeth C. Mansfield, 7th Edition 2013, Pearson

African-American Art (Oxford History of Art)

Sharon F. Patton, 1998, Oxford University Press

50 Contemporary Women Artists: Groundbreaking Contemporary Art from 1960 to Now

John Gosslee and Heather Zises, Editors, Foreword by Elizabeth Sackler, 2018 , Schiffer Publishing

How to Buy Art: A Beginner's Cheat Sheet

New York Times, William Grimes and Robin Pogrebin, May 7, 2015

How to Buy Art: A Beginner's Cheat Sheet

https://www.nytimes.com/2015/05/08/arts/design/how-to-buy-art-a-beginners-cheat-sheet.html

How to Hang Art Like a Professional

Architectural Digest, Amanda Sims, December 18, 2016

How to Hang Like a Professional

https://www.architecturaldigest.com/story/our-guide-to-hanging-art-like-a-professional

The Magic of Modern Art Tour

Go to a modern art exhibit.
Re-presence your declaration to be open to modern art.
Have in mind the new context you created.
Leave analysis and judgment at the door.

Find a peaceful spot and take a few minutes to breathe.
Look around and get an overall impression of the show.
Select a work you don't like at first.
Decide how long you'll spend with it (15-30 minutes).

Explore the piece from various angles and distances.
- Notice how it looks from various vantage points.
- Do your responses to it change as you move?

Get settled into a spot where you can easily see the whole piece.
Remain there as you immerse yourself in the work for the allotted time.
- Observe your thoughts.
- Observe your emotions.
- Observe your bodily sensations.

At the end of the time, ask yourself:
- Does the work seem any different now?
- How is it different (if it is)?
- What do you now see about it?
- What are you experiencing?
- What did you discover?

Debrief with someone or record your thoughts.
Repeat the process with a new piece.
Enjoy the rest of the exhibit.

Your experience is completely valid, and, in fact, perfect!

APPENDIX B: ALTERNATE APPROACHES – OTHER MODERN ART TOURS TO TRY

Describing What You See and What You Experience

Is it a two-dimensional or three-dimensional work?

What shape or shapes comprise it?

Are the shapes geometric or organic?

Does this work of art resemble something recognizable?

If so, how realistic does it look?

If it doesn't resemble anything recognizable, describe the
way it looks.

What is the scale of this piece?

Does it represent something from life?

If so, is it life-size, larger-than-life or smaller than the thing it
represents?

Does it make you want to look at it from far back or up close?

What is the medium?

Oil on canvas?

Welded metal?

Carved wood?

Mixed media?

Other?

What is the color scheme?

Is there a broad range of colors or a limited palette?

Are the colors mostly light or dark, brilliant or subdued?

Is there a lot of contrast?

Do the colors overlap?

How is the paint (or other material) applied?

Does it appear to have been applied quickly or slowly?

Is it thick, roughly textured or smooth?

Is the finish shiny or matte?

Are there visible brushstrokes?

Are the brushstrokes translucent or opaque?

What path do your eyes follow as you look at the piece?

Do your eyes move quickly or slowly?

Does your gaze want to move outside the piece or does it stay
within its boundaries?

Do your eyes keep returning to a focal point?

**What do you observe about the composition (design) of this
piece?**

Is it symmetrical or asymmetrical?

Does it have a feeling of balance or imbalance?

Are the shapes or lines confined within the overall piece or do
they go outside the borders?

Busy or minimalistic?

What is the overall feeling or mood of the piece?

Does it feel settled or unsettled?

Does it seem orderly or chaotic?

How do you feel as you explore this work of art?

**What do you think the piece is about or is intended to
communicate?**

Does it seem to be expressing a certain point of view?

When you look at it, does it remind you of anything?

How are you left after interacting with this piece?

Has it provoked memories?

Do you find yourself in a different mood?

What do you notice about your energy level?

Are you left thinking about the piece itself?

Do you feel like your creativity has been stimulated?

APPENDIX B: ALTERNATE APPROACHES – OTHER MODERN ART TOURS TO TRY

Entering the Artist's World

What did it take for the artist to bring this work from conception to completion?
    What might have been involved to produce this work of art?

What is the medium?
    Did the artist use the medium in a unique or unusual way?
    Why might the artist have chosen this medium?

If the work is very large, how might the artist have executed it?
    How did the artist position him or herself to work on it?
    Why might the artist have chosen to work on such a large scale?
    What could the artist have wanted to convey by working so large?

If the work is very small, how might the artist have executed it?
    How did the artist position him or herself to work on it?
    Why might the artist have chosen to work on such a small scale?
    What could the artist have wanted to convey by working so small?

How much time does it appear to have taken to create this piece?
    What do you think the difference in experience is for an artist to work on something for many days as opposed to going from start to finish in a short period of time?
    What does it tell you about the type of person the artist is likely to be?

What is the texture of the surface?
    How, and with what tools, might the artist have created that texture?
    How might the artist have moved his or her hand, arm or whole body to produce such a texture?

    What could the artist have intended to express through this choice of texture?
    If there is more than one texture, ask yourself these same questions for each one.

What kinds of colors are used for this piece?
    What might the artist's decision to use a limited palette or broad range of colors tell us about the artist's state of mind?
    Do the color choices seem to express a particular mood?
    What might all these color choices indicate about how the artist was feeling?

If the work looks particularly complex or particularly simple, how did the artist get it to look that way?
    What might this quality communicate about the artist's personality or nature?
    What could the artist have wanted to convey by choosing a simple or complex composition?

What is the overall feeling or mood of the piece?
    What might the artist have been feeling while creating this work of art?

What other questions or explorations come to mind about the artist's experience in creating this work of art?

APPENDIX C: ABOUT THE ART PROS WHO WERE INTERVIEWED FOR THIS BOOK

Who They Are in the Art World*

Aloma Marquis: Artist, Retired Professor, Stephen F. Austin University
Nacogdoches, Texas

Anthony Schmitt: Artist, Interior and Lighting Designer
Santa Monica, California

Barry Whistler: Gallery Owner, Barry Whistler Gallery
Dallas, Texas

Becky Hendrick: Artist, Author, Retired Instructor at Ball State University
Tucson, Arizona

Bob Adams: Artist, Adjunct Professor, Mesa Community College and Grand Canyon University
Phoenix, Arizona

Chris Cowden: Executive Director, Women & Their Work
Austin, Texas

Corrina Sephora: Artist
Atlanta, Georgia

Jamele Wright, Sr.: Artist, Art Professor, Clark University
Decatur, Georgia

Jonathan Tung: Gallery Owner, Art and Antiques Dealer
San Francisco, California and Austin, Texas

Joshua Kight: Artist, Art Teacher and Instructor, West Ridge Middle School, University of Texas and Austin Community College
Austin, Texas

Judith Simms: Senior Director, The Art School, The Contemporary Austin
Austin, Texas

Lawrence Oliverson: Fine Art Photographer
Sullivan, Wisconsin

Rachel Koper: Artist, Program Director, Women & Their Work
Austin, Texas

Rick Allred: Artist, Photographer, Photography Instructor
Santa Fe, New Mexico

Rohitash Rao: Artist, Designer, Illustrator, Videographer, Professor of Advertising Art, University of Texas
Austin Texas

Sally Weber: Artist
Oakland, California

Vincent Falsetta: Artist, Professor of Drawing and Painting, The University of North Texas
Denton, Texas

*Titles and professions are listed as they were at the time of the interviews.

Robyn Jamison is an artist on a mission—a mission to make the magic and wonder of Modern and Contemporary Art accessible to everyone in the world.

Robyn is a visual artist, published author, avid tap dancer and accomplished pianist. Holding a Master of Fine Arts degree from the University of North Texas, her artwork is in collections worldwide.

In retrospect, it's clear that everything in Robyn's life—including her artistic endeavors, her years of teaching, her passion for personal development—has proved to be the perfect preparation for her to fulfill her mission.

Robyn lives happily nestled in the hills of Austin, Texas, with her brainy, beloved husband and their adorable, quirky cats.

The following four pieces of art are the work of the author. She hopes you enjoy them!

To see more of her artwork, go to www.RobynJamison.com.

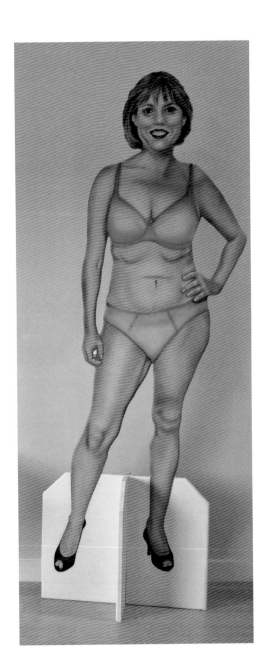
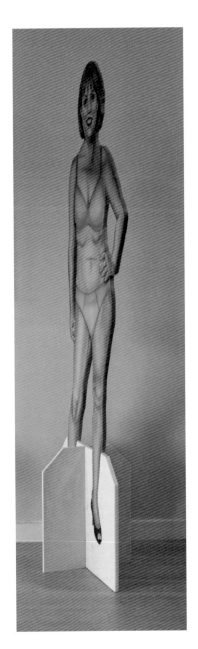

Robyn Jamison
She's a Doll
2021
    Acrylic on wood
27.5 x 82 x 18 inches
Courtesy of the Artist

Robyn Jamison
Downcast
1995
Charcoal on paper
38 x 50 inches
Courtesy of the Artist

ARTWORK BY THE AUTHOR

Robyn Jamison
Delicate Balance
2013
Photogravure à la poupée
8 x 10 inches
Courtesy of the Artist

Robyn Jamison
Tricycle Sentence
2019
Clayboard, graphite, acrylic sheet, ink
30.25 x 30.25 x 5.5 inches
Collection of Lorraine Telford